Research Report

T0303266

Understanding Low Survey Response Rates Among Young U.S. Military Personnel

Laura L. Miller, Eyal Aharoni

RAND Project AIR FORCE

Prepared for the United States Air Force
Approved for public release; distribution unlimited

RAND CORPORATION

For more information on this publication, visit www.rand.org/t/RR881

Library of Congress Control Number: 2015944865

ISBN: 978-0-8330-9017-1

Published by the RAND Corporation, Santa Monica, Calif.

Preface

This report documents research on survey nonresponse in U.S. military populations and U.S. populations more broadly, with special attention paid to younger age groups. In a 2012 survey of airmen conducted by the RAND Corporation for the Air Force Office of the Surgeon General (AF/SG), airmen in the youngest age group, ages 18 to 24, were the least likely to respond. Before analyzing the survey results, RAND researchers weighted the survey responses so that this group was represented proportionately in the analytic sample. The AF/SG was interested in possible reasons younger airmen were less likely to participate. Further examination of the 2012 survey revealed that junior enlisted airmen were less likely to respond than noncommissioned officers and other officers—including junior officers.

We reviewed response rates from other recent military surveys and U.S. survey response patterns more broadly to determine whether this lower rate among younger populations is common or unique to the 2012 RAND survey. Shaped by the availability of information for these surveys, *response rate* was defined very simply as the number of completed surveys divided by the number of invited participants. Thus, the nonrespondent category combines those who were unaware of the survey, those unable to access it, and those unable or unwilling to complete it.

Because the response-rate differences were not unique to the 2012 RAND survey, we explored possible explanations for the observed differences across age groups in surveys in general and made recommendations to encourage or facilitate the participation of young airmen in future surveys. The primary intended audiences for this report are U.S. Department of Defense (DoD) organizations that sponsor survey research and consume the survey results. This report might also interest researchers who administer such surveys.

The research reported here was commissioned by the AF/SG and conducted within the Manpower, Personnel, and Training Program of RAND Project AIR FORCE as part of a fiscal year 2014 project "Understanding Problematic Internet Use, and Using Information and Communication Technologies to Enhance Mental Health Support and Treatment." The results of the survey that led to this research were published in 2014 in *Information and Communication Technologies to Promote Social and Psychological Well-Being in the Air Force: A 2012 Survey of Airmen* (Miller et al., 2014). Also produced under the FY 2014 project was *A Review of Research on Problematic Internet Use and Well-Being: With Recommendations for the U.S. Air Force* (Breslau et al., 2015).

RAND Project AIR FORCE

RAND Project AIR FORCE (PAF), a division of the RAND Corporation, is the U.S. Air Force's federally funded research and development center for studies and analyses. PAF provides the Air Force with independent analyses of policy alternatives affecting the development, employment, combat readiness, and support of current and future air, space, and cyber forces. Research is conducted in four programs: Force Modernization and Employment; Manpower, Personnel, and Training; Resource Management; and Strategy and Doctrine. The research reported here was prepared under contract FA7014-06-C-0001.

Additional information about PAF is available on our website:

http://www.rand.org/paf

The draft report, issued on July 29, 2014, was reviewed by formal peer reviewers and U.S. Air Force subject-matter experts.

Contents

Tables and Figure

Summary

Survey researchers often seek to draw conclusions about a population based on responses from a smaller sample of people in the target population. Given this aim, it is important that survey participants accurately reflect the makeup of the population being studied. Survey researchers typically seek a high response rate among those invited to participate and hope to avoid a nonresponse bias, which occurs when the responses of those who participate in the survey differ in relevant and significant ways from how nonparticipants would have answered. This bias can limit the ability to generalize the findings to the entire population of study. High response rates, however, do not necessarily mean that the data are free from nonresponse bias, and low response rates do not mean that the data are biased. Many methodological strategies have been developed to assess, prevent, or mitigate nonresponse bias, but no strategy can guarantee that a sample will be entirely bias-free.

In 2012, the RAND Corporation conducted a survey on the role that information and communication technologies (ICTs), such as email, video chat, and the Internet, play in airmen's social and psychological well-being (Miller et al., 2014). Despite inviting a random sample of airmen to participate, and ICT use being the greatest among young adults, airmen ages 18 to 24 were underrepresented prior to weighting the results. This is a concern because this age range represents a large portion of the Air Force—namely, about one-third of the active-duty population.[1] Drilling down into the data revealed that this lack of participation was an issue among junior enlisted airmen but not junior officers. Underrepresentation was far less pronounced or absent among older, higher-ranking airmen. Partial surveys excluded from the analyses were more likely to come from active-duty airmen, junior enlisted personnel, and 18- to 24-year-olds than from other airmen.

This report was prepared for the Air Force Office of the Surgeon General in an effort to understand the lower response rates among younger airmen. Toward this effort, we examined the extent of age- or rank-related nonresponse in seven large military online survey studies. We found that younger service members, particularly younger enlisted personnel, tend to have the lowest response rates in recent military online survey research. Possible explanations include technological and situational barriers, as well as motivational factors, such as invitees' trust of the survey sponsor and interest in the topic.

---

[1] *Active duty* can include guard and reserve members serving on active duty, but, in this report, as in many U.S. Department of Defense (DoD) surveys and survey reports, the term *active duty* refers only to personnel from the active component. Active-duty guard and reserve members are included in the *guard* and *reserve* categories.

Recommendations

As survey response rates in the United States have been declining, surveyors have taken many steps to bolster response rates. However, it is unclear whether the focus on high response rates adds value, reduces nonresponse bias, and is worth the increase in survey costs. There is no set scientific standard for a minimal response rate for a survey to be valid. Scholars have demonstrated that high response rates can still contain bias, and some studies find the same survey results when low and high response rates are compared. For these reasons, this report does not focus simply on recommending strategies for increasing response rates: They might not necessarily fix any biases that exist and could actually exacerbate them. Instead, we conclude that the military should seek ways to better understand how well its surveys are capturing a representative sample of the chosen population. More specifically, we recommend additional efforts to identify factors potentially contributing to nonresponse bias so that survey sponsors invest only in strategies that would actually target the source of the problem rather than those that could just end up increasing participation among the types of people already well represented in the survey.

Air Force efforts to address the challenge and implications of lower response rates of military samples, and young members in particular, should consider the following recommendations. Our first recommendations for further research are in line with U.S. Government Accountability Office recommendations for DoD and with recommendations by the National Research Council for survey research more broadly, and thus could apply to other military surveys as well.

Explore Reasons Behind Nonresponse

Is nonresponse related to access, work overload, survey features, topic interest, attitudes toward the organization, attitudes toward surveys in general, privacy concerns, or other issues? Answers to this question could be explored both systematically and scientifically through research, but requests for feedback could also be conducted less formally through town-hall meetings, where senior leaders (such as major-command leaders) meet with junior enlisted and junior officer airmen without other members of their chains of command present.

Examine Whether Nonresponse Among Younger Airmen Reflects Lower Rates of Beginning a Survey or Lower Rates of Completing a Survey

Survey breakoff (that is, starting but not finishing a survey) among younger or lower-ranking airmen could be due to the survey length, item complexity, subject matter, or judgment-intensive items rather than lesser access to the Internet or initial unwillingness to participate in a survey. If younger or enlisted airmen are more likely to drop out mid-survey, survey analysts could conduct sensitivity analyses to determine whether decisions about defining surveys as completed (e.g., 50 percent of items or more) and constructing the subsequent survey weights have an impact on the outcomes of interest. Also, survey designers could consider placing items believed to be related to age and officer/enlisted status at the front of the survey.

Consider Additional Strategies to Increase Response Rates That Could Benefit the Air Force in Other Ways

The Air Force is already attempting to reduce the number of surveys it administers and limit overlap. Additional strategies to increase response rates might be worth the investment if they would provide value in other ways as well. For example, ensuring that all airmen have routine access at work to their Air Force email accounts could not only increase their opportunities to participate in surveys; it could also increase their opportunities to access important information provided by Air Force leadership and health professionals. Also, efforts to fill in missing contact information or correct erroneous addresses for airmen in the Air Force personnel data files could have similar benefits beyond addressing survey response rates.

Relatively low-cost approaches to increasing response rates and reducing data missingness might be worthwhile as strategies that could be employed in the near term, but we caution leaders that an increase in response rates does not necessarily mean that the results are representative. The survey sponsors could tailor recruitment emails to send to a random sample of junior officers and junior enlisted personnel and have the survey analysts use scientific methods to detect whether targeted appeals increase response rates relative to those from junior officers and junior enlisted personnel who do not receive targeted appeals. Language along the following lines might be appropriate for an Air Force survey:

> In recent years, leadership has noticed lower participation rates among young officer and young enlisted Airmen. You represent the future of the Air Force, and Air Force senior leaders want to make sure they have some insight into your experiences and opinions. Although senior leaders interact with young Airmen face to face, confidential surveys like these help them place those views into context. This is a voluntary survey: As you make your decision, we ask you to consider contributing to your Air Force in this way and encouraging your peers to participate as well so that the voices of young Airmen can be counted along with those of NCOs and more-senior officers.

If young airmen are less likely than other airmen to receive these invitations or read them, this language might make no difference in response rates. Similarly, it might not influence those who are cynical about or alienated from the organization and who might not take the message as genuine. But it is a relatively low-cost approach to try.

Do Not Invest Significant Resources in Efforts Solely to Increase Response Rates Across Air Force Surveys Without First Testing Whether There Is Any Value in Doing So

Response rates are not a sufficient metric for concluding whether survey results are representative of the views of the population. Demographic data can provide clues to the potential for bias and help to correct for it, but other factors not recorded in personnel databases could influence the decision or ability to participate in a survey.

Conduct Further Research to Test for Nonresponse Bias in Online Surveys

With strategies developed by survey researchers, analysts should assess whether lower response rates among the younger, junior officer, and junior enlisted personnel on major Air Force surveys result in nonresponse bias or low representation of those subgroups, despite weighting responses to make them demographically proportionate to the Air Force.

Survey administrators should experiment with sending paper surveys as follow-ups to nonrespondents, then analyze whether the responses of those who reply by mail differ significantly from those who responded online. Questions added to the end of the paper survey could assess whether Internet access, privacy issues, or other reasons explain nonresponse, which could inform future efforts to reduce barriers to participation (e.g., increasing computer availability to certain populations during Air Force headquarters survey periods).

The Air Force should also examine whether those who are last to participate in a survey tend to respond differently from those who respond early on; late responders might offer views somewhat similar to those who do not participate at all.

Make Surveys Mobile-Friendly

Given the explosion of smartphone and computer tablet use particularly among younger adults, researchers conducting surveys on behalf of DoD should consider designing shorter surveys with those devices in mind. Surveys could focus on fewer, higher-priority topics, or surveys could become more frequent but each much less time-consuming. Redesigning surveys for mobile platforms would incur some expense, but these platforms might provide the best way to engage future generations in the survey feedback mechanisms for senior military leaders.

Acknowledgments

We would like to thank Nicole Gamez and James "Eddie" Thompson for providing response-rate information from the Air Force Survey Office on the 2012 Air Force Climate Survey and reviewing for accuracy our initial description of that survey. Similar thanks are owed to Air Force Lt Col Wendy Travis, Maj Mark Oliver, and Jisuk Park for providing 2013 Air Force Community Assessment Survey information from the Air Force Medical Operations Agency. Lt Col Richard Roberts facilitated our request to Air Force Services for permission to include the response rates for the 2010 Air Force Caring for People Survey. We also thank our project action officer, Col Tracy A. Neal-Walden, for her review of an earlier draft of this report. We appreciated the constructive, detailed feedback from Paul Rosenfeld from the Defense Manpower Data Center.

We thank Chaitra M. Hardison for helpful input in the early stages of this study, Robert A. Guffey for advice on table formatting, and Jonathan Martens for assistance in formatting tables and references. Fabiola Lopez also provided support with the list of references. We are grateful for the editorial assistance of Melissa Bauman, which improved the first complete draft of this manuscript, and Lisa Bernard, who edited the final version of the report. Additionally, we thank Ray Conley and Kirsten Keller for their helpful feedback on an earlier report draft. We also benefited greatly from thorough peer reviews by Bonnie Ghosh-Dastidar and Jeremy N. V. Miles.

Abbreviations

AAPOR	American Association for Public Opinion Research
AFMOA	Air Force Medical Operations Agency
AFPC	Air Force Personnel Center
AF/SG	Air Force Office of the Surgeon General
CAC	Common Access Card
DMDC	Defense Manpower Data Center
DoD	U.S. Department of Defense
GAO	U.S. Government Accountability Office
ICT	information and communication technology
IDEAS	Interactive Demographic Analysis System
NCO	noncommissioned officer
NRC	National Research Council
OMB	Office of Management and Budget
SOFS	Status of Forces Survey

Chapter One. Response Rates on the 2012 RAND Survey of Airmen on Information and Communication Technologies and Well-Being

Background

Representative sampling is an important component of survey studies that aim to generalize to a broader population. However, in practice, representative distributions can be difficult to achieve because the various populations in a sample are not equally reached through recruitment strategies or equally willing and able to participate. Differences in response rates raise questions about how meaningful those differences are to the survey results. That is, would people who were either unwilling or unable to participate have responded to the survey questions differently from those who did participate, creating a nonresponse bias in the results?

Differences between the characteristics of participants and nonparticipants are relevant for representation only if they are tied to a survey's topics. For example, if a military survey is assessing satisfaction with services on military installations, and officers and enlisted personnel are equally likely to be satisfied with those facilities, then it does not matter whether one of those groups is more likely than the other to participate in the survey. The survey respondents could be 100 percent enlisted personnel and the reported satisfaction levels would still be representative of the military population. If, however, officers are much more likely to participate in the survey and are much more likely to be satisfied with the services, then the survey results will not give an accurate picture of the attitudes of the military population as a whole.

Researchers can and typically do correct for these types of differences using observed characteristics, such as officer/enlisted status. However, some differences in response rates might result from factors that were never measured. For example, if airmen who are satisfied with their commanders are less likely than dissatisfied airmen to participate in the Air Force Climate Survey because they feel they have no complaints, then the survey might produce an overly negative picture of command climate across the Air Force. Unlike differences in response rates associated with officer/enlisted status, there is no known ratio of satisfied and unsatisfied airmen that researchers could use to weight the survey data so they could accurately represent the force. The potential for this type of hidden bias to distort leadership's understanding of its personnel is the primary concern of this report.

2012 RAND Survey

To help the Air Force understand the role that information and communication technologies (ICTs), such as email, video chat, and the Internet, play in airmen's social and psychological well-being, in 2012, RAND researchers conducted a web-based survey of active-duty, guard, and reserve airmen.[1] The web-based survey is a relatively low-cost option that permits airmen to take the survey when and where it is convenient for them, and the data are immediately available in an electronic database. The RAND team and the research sponsor had hoped that the ICT portion of the research topic might interest airmen, in part because American adults younger than 50 are enthusiastic adopters of technology (see Fox and Rainie, 2014) and in part because it was an uncommon topic in major Air Force and U.S. Department of Defense (DoD) surveys. Research has shown that survey topic interest can influence survey participation decisions (Groves, Presser, and Dipko, 2004).

The RAND team found a substantial discrepancy in age between the airmen invited to participate in this survey and the airmen who actually completed it, defined as reaching the end of the survey.[2] Airmen ages 35 and older were overrepresented among survey respondents in our analytic sample compared with their proportion of the Air Force population, and airmen ages 18 to 34 were underrepresented. Although a sufficient sample size for the planned analyses was obtained and the analytic sample was weighted to match the age distribution in the Air Force before the survey results were analyzed, the Air Force Office of the Surgeon General (AF/SG) expressed concern about the willingness of the youngest airmen (ages 18 to 24) to participate. Our objective for this follow-on report is to identify possible age-related trends in online survey response rates to improve future web-based surveys aiming to sample military populations.

This chapter first provides an overview of the sampling strategy for the 2012 survey of airmen on ICT and well-being. It then presents the survey response rates for active-duty, guard, and reserve airmen by age group and by rank group. The chapter concludes with the research questions that shaped further consideration of the relevance of these response rates, and the organization for the remainder of this report.

---

[1] RAND's institutional review board, the Human Subjects Protection Committee, approved the conduct of this research. RAND also received the required approvals from the Air Force Manpower Agency, which issues the Air Force survey control numbers; from the Air Force Research Oversight and Compliance Office, whose review functioned as a second board review; and from the Air Force Chief Information Office, which granted a waiver for us to host an Air Force survey on a nonmilitary (i.e., not .mil) website. We present the survey results in a separate report (Miller et al., 2014).

[2] Whereas the Defense Manpower Data Center's (DMDC's) response rates typically include the percentage of people who complete 50 percent or more of the survey, the RAND team considered anything less than reaching the end of the survey as having submitted only a partial survey. Because the survey was truly anonymous, if we had included partial surveys, we would have risked double-counting people who started the survey and then returned more than three days later to complete it and had to begin again. To meet the requirements of our human subjects protection review, responses were sealed after three days to protect against others being able to view them.

Survey Sampling Strategy

Concerned that airmen were becoming oversurveyed, the Air Force asked that survey researchers help reduce the burden on airmen. The RAND team sought to minimize the number of airmen invited to participate yet ensure enough respondents for the purposes of the study. Recognizing that survey response rates are a challenge in military populations, we calculated that one-third of invited airmen might participate. Because ICT usage patterns might vary by certain demographic characteristics, such as age, sex, and rank, and by whether airmen were active duty, guard, or reserve, we wanted to ensure that the analytic sample would include enough of the different subgroups to permit statistical analyses of differences.

Calculations first revealed that a simple random sample of airmen that was large enough to recruit the desired number of guard and reserve airmen in each of the gender, age-group, and rank-group categories would recruit far more active-duty airmen than necessary. So we drew an initial random sample of 4,500 airmen from each of the service-status populations (active duty, guard, and reserve), with the intention of weighting the survey responses to reflect their actual proportions in the Air Force (a population that, in 2012, contained 65 percent active-duty, 21 percent guard, and 14 percent reserve airmen).[3] This strategy would produce enough respondents for every subgroup but one: active-duty airmen ages 45 and older. Therefore, rather than greatly increase the number of invitations just to acquire enough airmen in that one subgroup, that population was strategically oversampled (we sent an additional 437 invitations to them). Oversampling also addressed the concern that this subgroup might be less likely to respond because it is disproportionately made up of senior officers who have remained beyond the 20-year retirement mark.[4] However, the opposite turned out to be true. This subgroup was actually more likely to respond than younger airmen and thus was not oversampled when we drew an additional random sample toward the end of the survey period to ensure sufficient sample sizes for the planned analyses. In total, we sent invitations to 9,437 active-duty airmen, 9,000 guard airmen, and 9,000 reserve airmen. Appendix A provides detailed information about strategies employed to promote participation in the 2012 RAND survey of airmen on ICT and well-being. Appendix B presents the template for the invitation for that survey.

Response Rates, Demographic Composition of the Survey Sample, and the 2012 Air Force Population

Airmen across the different subgroups were not equally likely to participate in the survey. As mentioned, the AF/SG was particularly concerned about the especially low rate among airmen

---

[3] For additional details on the sample and weighting methods, see Appendix C in Miller et al., 2014.

[4] At the time of the sample design, officers made up 63 percent of active-duty airmen ages 45 or older but just 19 percent of active-duty airmen overall.

ages 18 to 24 (see Table 1.1)—and not because of the impact on this one survey. The AF/SG wondered whether younger airmen—the future of the Air Force—were less likely to give Air Force leadership their perspectives through participation in official surveys. As seen in Table 1.1, in the active-duty, guard, and reserve populations, response rates increased with each step up in age group. Although 9 percent of invited active-duty airmen ages 18 to 24 completed surveys, 29 percent of active-duty airmen ages 45 and older did. This uneven response rate resulted in a final survey sample that did not reflect the age distribution of the Air Force (e.g., the youngest age group made up 32 percent of the active-duty population in 2012 but just 16 percent of the active-duty survey sample). Partial surveys excluded from both the analyses and the response rates reported in Table 1.1 were more likely to have come from active-duty airmen, junior enlisted personnel, and 18- to 24-year-olds than from their counterparts. Because we could not link responses to individuals, we do not know whether this population was more likely to drop out of the survey entirely or just more likely to have to restart the survey because of interruptions while taking it.

Table 1.1 Response Rates, Percentage of Total Respondents, and 2012 Population Rates of Airmen, by Age Group

	Active Duty			Air National Guard			Air Force Reserve		
Age Group	Response Rate (%)	Percentage of Total Respondents (N = 1,634)	Percentage of 2012 Population (N = 328,667)	Response Rate (%)	Percentage of Total Respondents (N = 977)	Percentage of 2012 Population (N = 104,751)	Response Rate (%)	Percentage of Total Respondents (N = 868)	Percentage of 2012 Population (N = 70,996)
18–24[a]	9	16	32	4	6	17	3	4	15
25–34	17	41	44	8	25	35	6	24	35
35–44	25	29	21	12	32	28	11	32	27
45+	29	14	4	19	38	21	17	41	23

SOURCE: We obtained the population distribution from the Air Force Personnel Center's (AFPC's) Interactive Demographic Analysis System (IDEAS) in February 2012. It does not include general officers, which are less than 1 percent of the population.

NOTE: We sent approximately half the survey invitations more than one month into the survey administration period, which boosted the respondent pool but likely limited overall response rates because of the truncated response window. Blue shading indicates the youngest and generally least-likely-to-respond group.

[a] Actual Air Force population subgroup is ages 17 to 24, but we excluded minors from our survey.

The Air Force structure is hierarchical, and people typically enter the military at either the junior enlisted or the junior officer ranks and progress to the higher ranks through the years of service. There is no lateral entry into the highest ranks of the military from the civilian sector, and those who enter in the middle have accumulated education and possibly professional experience prior to joining. Given this design, age and rank in the military are closely, positively related. For this follow-on study, we examined the survey response rates by rank group as well. Table 1.2 shows that the lower response rate among young airmen is actually more concentrated among junior enlisted airmen (9 percent for active-duty E-1 to E-4s, and 4 percent for guard and reserves) than among young officers (17 percent for active-duty O-1 to O-3s, and 11 percent and 10 percent for guard and reserves, respectively). Consequently, although airmen in pay grades E-1 to E-4 made up 37 percent of the 2012 active-duty population, they made up 20 percent of our unweighted sample of active-duty respondents. Reflecting the increasing response rates by age group above was the increased likelihood that airmen who have made the military a career and reached the higher enlisted and officer ranks (E-7 to E-9 and O-4 to O-6) would respond to the survey over airmen early in their careers.

Table 1.2 Response Rates, Percentage of Total Respondents, and 2012 Population Rates of Airmen, by Rank Group

	Active Duty			Air National Guard			Air Force Reserve		
Rank Group	Response Rate (%)	Percentage of Total Respondents (N = 1,634)	Percentage of 2012 Population (N = 328,812)	Response Rate (%)	Percentage of Total Respondents (N = 977)	Percentage of 2012 Population (N = 105,389)	Response Rate (%)	Percentage of Total Respondents (N = 868)	Percentage of 2012 Population (N = 71,428)
E-1 to E-4	9	20	37	4	10	27	4	11	29
E-5 to E-6	17	32	33	10	36	38	9	31	33
E-7 to E-9	34	20	10	19	37	21	16	30	18
O-1 to O-3	17	11	11	11	5	5	10	6	6
O-4 to O-6	32	17	9	14	11	9	15	21	14
O-7 to O-10	59[a]	<1	<1	11[a]	<1	<1	67[a]	<1	<1

SOURCE: Population distribution from Office of the Deputy Assistant Secretary of Defense for Military Community and Family Policy (2013, pp. 17, 62).
NOTE: We sent approximately half the survey invitations more than one month into the survey administration period, which boosted the respondent pool but likely limited overall response rates because of the truncated response window.
[a] Represents very small numbers, so one or two people can change these percentages dramatically.

These findings highlight the potential importance of the standard practice of weighting the survey responses to reflect the composition of the Air Force population before analyzing the results, to avoid the older leadership being overrepresented and skewing the overall picture for survey topics correlated with age. We did address the potential for nonresponse bias by weighting the survey results with regard to gender, age group, officer/enlisted status, and affiliation (active duty, guard, or reserve) relative to the Air Force population before analyses. The question relevant to this survey and surveys in general—even those that achieve proportionate responses across subgroups—is whether those who did not complete the survey would have answered the questions differently from those who did.

Research Questions

In a purely random sample, in which everyone is equally likely to receive a survey invitation and equally likely to respond, the distribution of the survey respondents should approximate the distribution of the population. The overresponse of the older age group and the marked underresponse of young and enlisted airmen raised the following questions, which we explore in turn:

- *Other surveys:* Were these findings anomalous? What is the relationship between age or rank and response rates in other surveys of military populations? Are response rates lower among young American adults in general?
- *Explanatory factors:* Why might younger airmen have been less likely than older airmen to complete the 2012 RAND survey? Why might younger enlisted airmen have been less likely than young officers to complete one?
- *Implications:* What are the implications of lower response rates among certain subgroups? Do they mean that the survey results are biased?
- *Response:* What additional strategies, if any, should the Air Force consider to increase the response rates of younger adults or young enlisted personnel in future Air Force surveys? Are they necessary?

Organization of This Report

Chapter Two explores reported response rates by age group or rank group in seven other large surveys of military populations, with particular focus on three large surveys of U.S. Air Force personnel. Chapter Three explores current survey research approaches to understanding low response rates and assessing and addressing nonresponse bias. Chapter Four highlights the study's conclusions and offers recommendations for Air Force surveys that could apply to DoD surveys more broadly. Appendix A describes strategies used to promote survey participation in the 2012 survey. Appendix B provides the invitation sent to participate in that survey.

Chapter Two. Response Patterns by Age or Rank Group in Other Large Recent Surveys of U.S. Military Personnel

In this chapter, we explore whether other large surveys of Air Force personnel and military personnel more broadly have experienced similar response patterns to those of the 2012 RAND survey of airmen on ICT and well-being. DoD-sponsored surveys of military personnel differ in terms of survey topic, targeted population, sample size, participant recruitment strategies, survey sponsor, mode of administration, name recognition, and other characteristics. However, if younger enlisted military personnel in general are less able to, less interested in, or less willing to participate in DoD- or service-sponsored surveys, we might find similar patterns despite the variation. In fact, such a pattern emerged.

Comparison of Response Rates Across Large U.S. Department of Defense Surveys

To provide context for the 2012 RAND survey, we selected seven major surveys comparable according to several criteria. We identified surveys of U.S. military personnel that were sponsored by an organization within DoD. Thus we have limited the comparison to surveys sponsored by the sample's employer and targeting a similar population. Our selection focused on large-scale surveys that similarly attempt to sample geographically dispersed service members from across a service or DoD. We did not collect information on the innumerable smaller surveys of specific populations (e.g., unit surveys, installation surveys, postdeployment surveys, or satisfaction surveys of users of specific programs), in part for practical reasons, but also because of the diminished degree of comparability. Additionally, because response rates for online surveys are typically lower than those for paper surveys administered in person or by mail (Dillman, Smyth, and Christian, 2009), we limited our selection to surveys that were administered online (although we did not rule out a survey if it offered a paper alternative to the web-based primary version). To control for temporal variation, we focused on surveys conducted from 2010 to 2012, or within two years of the RAND survey. We were unable to include some surveys, such as the 2010 Navy Pregnancy and Parenthood Survey, because response rates by age or rank were not available.

The selected surveys include the three largest surveys of Air Force personnel, three DoD surveys, and an Army survey. Because these are all recurring surveys, the 2010-to-2012 time frame allowed us to include the most recent one with response-rate data available to us. An in-depth, comprehensive review of the large surveys, their methodologies, their means for calculating response rates, historical trends, and details about their response rates was beyond the scope of this study. The purpose of our high-level review of surveys was to identify, from readily available sources, whether there might be a pattern of lower response rates among young or enlisted military personnel that would warrant further consideration.

We collected information on overall response rates and response differences based on what was available for either age subgroups or rank subgroups. Unless otherwise noted, *response rate* was defined simply as the number of respondents in an age or rank group divided by the total number of survey invitees. In surveys conducted by DMDC, response rates are weighted to adjust for disproportionate sampling. Note that the American Association for Public Opinion Research (AAPOR) has developed standard definitions for survey response rates that take into account such factors as whether participants provided only partial or completed surveys, whether invitees actively refused to participate, whether invitees were unable to participate (e.g., deceased or hospitalized), and whether the contact information for invitees was inaccurate (AAPOR, 2011). This level of detail was not available for most surveys reviewed, so it is important to keep in mind that response rates reported here should not be interpreted solely as an indicator of willingness to participate. Among those not counted as respondents would be service members who did not receive the survey announcement or invitation and service members who were unable to participate.

Response rates are reported alongside the corresponding composition of survey respondents and the population prevalence (the number of service members in a corresponding age or rank group divided by the total number of service members in that category during the year of the survey). The total population figures include both those who would and those who would not have been invited to participate in the survey. A descriptive comparison of these data can offer insight into the direction of divergence from the population rate. In the following sections, we describe how response rates by age or rank group were derived for each survey. We begin our review with three major Air Force–wide surveys, each administered on an Air Force website, and then move to three other surveys of military personnel conducted in this time frame. For the reasons described in Appendix A, the lower response rate overall for the 2012 RAND survey relative to these surveys was not unexpected and is not the focus here. Rather, we examined these response rates to identify whether young or junior enlisted service members appeared to be less likely to participate in these surveys than officers or older service members.

Air Force Surveys

Air Force Community Assessment Survey, 2013

The Air Force Community Assessment Survey is a recurring survey designed to help Air Force leadership determine the installation-specific needs of Air Force communities and to inform service planning and resource allocation. The results are intended to "assist helping professionals working in chaplains' offices, Airman and family readiness centers, family advocacy programs, health and wellness centers, mental health clinics and child and youth programs to better meet the needs of service members and their families" (AFPC, 2011). The topics included "personal and family adjustment, individual and family adaptation, community well-being, deployment, resiliency, post-traumatic stress and help-seeking stigma" (AFPC, 2011). Participants included active-duty, reserve, and guard airmen, selected through a stratified random sampling approach designed to solicit sufficient levels of participation from each installation.[1] The online survey was estimated to take about 30 minutes to complete.

The overall response rate for active-duty airmen on this 2013 survey was 24 percent. Table 2.1 shows the percentage of the active-duty population invited to participate in the survey in 2013 and response rates for each active-duty rank group. We obtained the population prevalence for each rank for 2013 from the AFPC IDEAS database (see AFPC, 2012), which includes both those invited and those not invited to participate in the survey. The different rank groups were similarly sampled, with a slightly higher percentage of officers being sampled (65 percent of O-1 to O-3s and 63 percent of O-4s and above) than of enlisted airmen (about 60 percent).

Table 2.1 shows that the lowest survey response rates (12 percent) were among junior enlisted airmen (E-1s to E-4s)—which is the largest rank group in the Air Force at 36 percent of the population. Response rates were highest among older career airmen: Forty-three percent of senior noncommissioned officers (NCOs) (E-7s to E-9s) and 40 percent of higher-ranking officers (O-4s to O-10s) participated in the survey.

Table 2.1 Response Rates by Rank Group for the 2013 Air Force Community Assessment Survey: Active Duty

Rank Group	Response Rate (%)	Percentage of Total Respondents	Percentage of Total Population
E-1 to E-4	12	17	36
E-5 to E-6	26	37	33
E-7 to E-9	43	19	11
O-1 to O-3	24	12	11
O-4+	40	15	8

SOURCES: Response rates and total respondents: Air Force Medical Operations Agency (AFMOA). Population rate: AFPC IDEAS.
NOTE: N = 34,909.

The overall response rate for guard and reserve airmen was 14 percent. Table 2.2 shows that the same response pattern for active-duty airmen shown in Table 2.1 can be observed for guard and reserve airmen, with the higher response rates appearing among higher-tenure airmen and participation among E-1s to E-4s being particularly low (5 percent).

[1] Air Force civilians and spouses are also invited to participate, but those populations were outside the scope of this review.

Table 2.2 Response Rates by Rank Group for the 2013 Air Force Community Assessment Survey: Guard and Reserve

Rank Group	Response Rate (%)	Percentage of Total Respondents	Percentage of Total Population
E-1 to E-4	5	9	30
E-5 to E-6	12	28	34
E-7 to E-9	26	38	20
O-1 to O-3	11	6	5
O-4+	20	18	11

SOURCES: Response rates and total respondents: AFMOA. Population rate: AFPC IDEAS.
NOTE: N = 10,725.

Air Force Climate Survey, 2012

The Air Force Climate Survey is a census survey given every two years that is designed to assess opinions about job satisfaction, trust in leadership, work environment, unit performance, recognition, and resources among active-duty, guard, and reserve airmen.[2] With a few exceptions (namely, students, prisoners, and personnel on medical hold), every airman assigned to an unclassified unit and who had an official email address and a Common Access Card (CAC) (a DoD identity card) was invited to take the survey. The online survey was estimated to take about 20 minutes to complete.

The Air Force Survey Office provided the response rates overall and for each rank. These rates are completion rates: the number of respondents in a category divided by the total population invited for that category, with the denominator adjusted to remove the number of email invitations that were undeliverable. In 2012, the overall response rate for Air Force military personnel was 28 percent. The response rates were 31 percent, 26 percent, and 20 percent for invited active-duty, guard, and reserve airmen, respectively.

Table 2.3 presents the 2012 survey response rates, total respondents, and population rates by rank for active-duty airmen, and Table 2.4 shows those rates for guard and reserve airmen. Note that, unlike response rates and percentage of total respondents, the total population figures include airmen who would not have been eligible for or invited to take the survey. The data in Table 2.3 show that junior enlisted airmen have the lowest response rates among the active-duty ranks. Within that group, E-3s have the highest response rate at 27 percent and E-1s the lowest at 19 percent (not shown). Most pay grades above E-4 participated in the survey at higher rates than those of junior enlisted airmen.

[2] Air Force civilians are also invited to participate, but those populations were outside the scope of this review.

Table 2.3 Response Rates by Rank for the 2012 Air Force Climate Survey: Active Duty

Rank	Response Rate (%)	Percentage of Total Respondents	Percentage of Total Population
E-1 to E-4	25	27	37
E-5 to E-6	32	38	34
E-7 to E-9	41	15	11
O-1 to O-3	30	10	11
O-4+	35	10	8

SOURCES: Response rates and total respondents: AFPC. Population rates: Office of the Deputy Assistant Secretary of Defense for Military Community and Family Policy (2013, pp. 17, 62).
NOTE: N = 86,505.

Table 2.4 Response Rates by Rank for the 2012 Air Force Climate Survey: Guard and Reserve

	Guard			Reserve		
Rank	Response Rate (%)	Percentage of Total Respondents	Percentage of Total Population	Response Rate (%)	Percentage of Total Respondents	Percentage of Total Population
E-1 to E-4	14	12	26	11	17	29
E-5 to E-6	23	40	38	16	32	33
E-7 to E-9	37	35	21	29	27	17
O-1 to O-3	19	4	5	14	6	6
O-4+	22	8	10	19	18	15

SOURCES: Response rates and total respondents: AFPC. Population rates: Office of the Deputy Assistant Secretary of Defense for Military Community and Family Policy (2013, pp. 17, 62).
NOTE: N = 22,771 for guard and 8,077 for reserve.

For the most part, guard and reserve airmen responded at lower rates than their active-duty counterparts did; as shown in Table 2.4, response rates tended to be highest among senior NCOs (E-7s to E-9s).

Air Force Caring for People Survey, 2010

The Caring for People survey is a recurring survey that solicits feedback about how Air Force leaders can better leverage existing services, programs, and facilities to enhance the health and well-being of airmen and their families. This survey is a census of the Air Force population that includes active-duty, guard, and reserve members.[3] Administered online, this survey was

[3] Air Force civilians, retirees, and spouses are also invited to participate, but those populations were outside the scope of this review.

estimated to take about 20 minutes to complete. The Air Force Survey Office had previously provided the 2010 survey data to RAND for another study (Meadows, Miller, and Miles, 2014); before destroying the data at the completion of the project, we obtained Air Force permission to compute response rates for these age groups for this report.

The overall response rate was approximately 15 percent for active-duty personnel and 8 percent for guard and reserve. As shown in Table 2.5, we combined age-group frequencies available from IDEAS for officer and enlisted populations and for reserve and guard as of the end of 2010.[4] Because this was a census survey, we computed response rates by dividing the number of survey respondents in each age group by the number of airmen in that age group in the Air Force population. As with the 2012 RAND survey (see Table 1.1 in Chapter One), the youngest age group was underrepresented among total respondents because of lower response rates.

Table 2.5 Response Rates by Age Group for the 2010 Air Force Caring for People Survey

	Active Duty			Guard and Reserve		
Age Group	Response Rate (%)	Percentage of Total Respondents	Percentage of Total Population	Response Rate (%)	Percentage of Total Respondents	Percentage of Total Population
≤24	9	19	32	2	3	15
25–34	15	42	42	5	22	34
35–44	22	31	22	10	34	29
≥45	29	8	4	15	41	22

SOURCES: Data to calculate response rates: Air Force Survey Office. Population rates: AFPC IDEAS.
NOTE: N = 65,254.

These three major Air Force surveys experienced some variation in response rates; however, the youngest airmen, particularly the junior enlisted airmen, tended to respond at lower rates than their counterparts did. A review of four other service and DoD surveys revealed that lower response rates among young military personnel, and among the junior enlisted in particular, are not limited to the Air Force.

[4] The Air Force IDEAS database does not include all general officers, who make up less than 1 percent of the Air Force population.

Other U.S. Department of Defense Surveys

U.S. Department of Defense 2012 Workplace and Gender Relations Surveys

In 2012, DMDC administered active and reserve component versions of a survey that addresses topics related to military life; the military workplace; stress, health, and well-being; gender-related discrimination and harassment; unwanted sexual contact; and military sexual assault prevention and response (DMDC, 2012f). The 2012 DoD Workplace and Gender Relations Survey of Active Duty Members was designed to include Army, Navy, Air Force, and Marine Corps personnel age 18 or older (excluding general and flag officers) who had at least six months of service (DMDC, 2013). DMDC employed a single-stage, nonproportional stratified random sampling approach, oversampling women (including sampling all women in the Marine Corps) and oversampling men in the Marine Corps (DMDC, 2012f). Oversampling Marine Corps personnel could have increased the number of junior enlisted in the final sample because a higher proportion of the active-duty Marine Corps is ranked E-1 to E-4 (59 percent) than of the Army (45 percent), Navy (42 percent), or Air Force (37 percent) (Office of the Deputy Assistant Secretary of Defense for Military Community and Family Policy, 2013, p. 17). The web-based survey administered by DMDC was estimated to take between 16 and 30 minutes to complete.

DMDC uses AAPOR definitions to prepare its response rates, which take into account such factors as missing contact information in personnel files, members who are no longer eligible (e.g., retired or deceased), and incomplete responses. Its reported response rates are defined as the number of usable responses divided by the adjusted eligible sample (DMDC, 2012f, p. 19; DMDC, 2012c, p. 15). Thus, the response rates reported here have already been weighted to account for disproportionate sampling.

The overall response rate for the active-duty survey was 24 percent (DMDC, 2012f). The first column in Table 2.6 shows that junior enlisted personnel in pay grades E-1 to E-4 were much less likely to respond than any other rank group, and this group made up 43 percent of the active-duty population. Comparing only officers, company-grade officers (O-1 to O-3) were less likely to respond than field-grade officers (O-4 to O-6).

Table 2.6 Response Rates by Rank for the 2012 Workplace and Gender Relations Survey of Active-Duty Members

Rank Group	Response Rate (%)	Percentage of Total Respondents	Percentage of Total Population
E-1 to E-3	12	20	23
E-4	14	16	20
E-5 to E-6	27	29	30
E-7 to E-9	43	11	10
W-1 to W-5	31	3	1[a]
O-1 to O-3	33	13	9
O-4 to O-6	46	8	6

SOURCES: Response rates and total respondents: DMDC, 2012f, p. 20. Population rate: Office of the Deputy Assistant Secretary of Defense for Military Community and Family Policy, 2013, p. 6.
NOTE: N = 22,792.
[a] Warrant officers were not reported separately in survey documentation but elsewhere are reported as 1 percent (Office of the Deputy Assistant Secretary of Defense for Military Community and Family Policy, 2013).

The 2012 DoD Workplace and Gender Relations Survey of Reserve Component Members used a single-stage, nonproportional stratified random sampling strategy (DMDC, 2012c). It stratified by gender, pay grade, reserve component (including the Coast Guard Reserve), and reserve program. As with the active-duty survey, it oversampled subgroups that were small or had low response rates.

The overall response rate for this web survey was 23 percent. Table 2.7 shows a response-rate pattern by pay grade similar to that in previous table.

Table 2.7 Response Rates by Rank for the 2012 Workplace and Gender Relations Survey of Reserve-Component Members

Rank Group	Response Rate (%)	Percentage of Total Respondents	Percentage of Total Population
E-1 to E-3	10	10	19
E-4	11	17	24
E-5 to E-6	25	27	30
E-7 to E-9	46	17	12
W-1 to W-5	41	3	1
O-1 to O-3	29	12	7
O-4 to O-6	43	14	7

SOURCES: Response rates and total respondents: DMDC, 2012c, p. 18. Population rate: Office of the Deputy Assistant Secretary of Defense for Military Community and Family Policy, 2013, p. 62.
NOTE: N = 15,250.

U.S. Department of Defense Status of Forces Surveys, 2012

The recurring DoD Status of Forces Surveys (SOFSs) assess the attitudes and opinions on personnel and policy issues, including job satisfaction, work stress, deployments, aspects of military life, well-being, retention intentions, and satisfaction with services provided by DoD. The surveys employ a stratified random sampling approach to solicit participation from Army, Navy, Air Force, and Marine Corps members. They are expected to take most respondents about 30 minutes to complete and are administered via the DoD website.

DMDC reported that, in 2008–2010, the response rates for these surveys ranged from 29 percent to 32 percent for active-duty personnel and from 25 percent to 29 percent for reserve-component personnel (DoD, 2010, p. 37). The overall response rate for the active-duty survey in June 2012 was 26 percent, and the Air Force had the highest response rate at 37 percent (DMDC, 2012d, p. 19). The overall survey response rate for the June 2012 guard and reserve populations in all services was 26 percent, and it was 39 percent for the Air National Guard and 31 percent for the Air Force Reserve (DMDC, 2012d, p. 19).

Sample response rates for each rank group on the June 2012 surveys were published by DMDC; as with the previous survey, the response rate is defined as the number of usable responses divided by the adjusted eligible sample (DMDC, 2012d, p. 19; DMDC, 2012e, p. 19). Table 2.8 presents the response rates, composition of the total respondent population, and the population rate for active-duty personnel. Service members ranking E-1 through E-4 responded at a rate of 13 percent, while other rank groups responded at more than double that rate.

Table 2.8 Response Rates by Rank for the 2012 Status of Forces Survey: Active Duty

Rank Group	Response Rate (%)	Percentage of Total Respondents	Percentage of Total Population
E-1 to E-4	13	20	39
E-5 to E-9	33	38	43
W-1 to W-5	38	4	1
O-1 to O-3	38	18	9
O-4 to O-6	54	20	7

SOURCES: Response rates: DMDC, 2012d, p. 19. Total respondents and population rate: DMDC, 2012a, p. 10.
NOTE: N = 15,423.

This pattern is also apparent in Table 2.9, which presents similar information for the combined guard and reserve populations, although DMDC provided a bit more granularity on the enlisted response rates for this group.

Table 2.9 Response Rates by Rank for the 2012 Status of Forces Survey: Guard and Reserve

Rank Group	Response Rate (%)	Percentage of Total Respondents	Percentage of Total Population
E-1 to E-3	10	19	39
E-4	12		
E-5 to E-6	28	36	45
E-7 to E-9	50		
W-1 to W-5	46	[a]	[a]
O-1 to O-3	36	19	7
O-4 to O-6	52	22	7

SOURCES: Response rates: DMDC, 2012e, p. 19. Total respondents and population rate: DMDC, 2012b, p. 10.
NOTE: N = 26,826.
[a] Warrant officers were not reported separately.

U.S. Department of Defense Health Related Behaviors Survey, 2011

The DoD Health Related Behaviors Survey of Active Duty Military Personnel is a recurring survey that assesses the nature, causes, and consequences of lifestyle health, safety, and substance-abuse patterns among active-duty service members to inform prevention and intervention policies and practices and promote the overall health and readiness of the force.

The 2011 survey recruited from the Army, Navy, Marine Corps, Air Force, and Coast Guard using a stratified random sampling approach. For the 2011 survey, the administration mode was switched from a paper-based, group-administered, in-person format to an online survey to reduce the burden on the units, cut survey administration costs, and expand the survey's geographic reach (DoD, 2013, p. ES-2). Invitation and reminder postcards were sent to the physical addresses of service members with no email addresses in the DMDC database, a population that tended to be concentrated among junior enlisted personnel (DoD, 2013, p. ES-3). After an assessment of the survey completion rates by the different demographic strata in the initial invited sample, invitations were sent to an additional sample selected from the demographic subgroups with particularly low response rates (DoD, 2013, p. 11). The survey was estimated to take about 40 minutes to complete.

Using the AAPOR response-rate definitions, the final overall response rate for the DoD portion of the sample, excluding the Coast Guard, was 22 percent; for the Air Force population, it was 33 percent (DoD, 2013, p. 20). DoD published response rates by pay grade, by gender, and by service (DoD, 2013, pp. 21–22); we combined them to report response rates by rank group for all of DoD (Table 2.10) and for the Air Force only (Table 2.11).

Table 2.10 Response Rates by Rank Group for the 2011 Health Related Behaviors Survey of Active-Duty Personnel: All U.S. Department of Defense

Rank Group	Response Rate (%)	Percentage of Total Respondents	Percentage of Total Population
E-1 to E-4	15	32	44
E-5 to E-6	35	28	29
E-7 to E-9	55	16	9
W-1 to W-5	36	4	1
O-1 to O-3	36	11	9
O-4+	55	9	6

SOURCES: Response rate and total respondents: DoD, 2013, pp. 21–23. Population rate: Office of the Deputy Under Secretary of Defense for Military Community and Family Policy, 2012, p. 15.
NOTE: N = 34,416.

Table 2.11 Response Rates by Rank Group for the 2011 Health Related Behaviors Survey of Active-Duty Personnel: Air Force Only

Rank Group	Response Rate (%)	Percentage of Total Respondents	Percentage of Total Population
E-1 to E-4	26	37	36
E-5 to E-6	39	28	34
E-7 to E-9	51	16	10
O-1 to O-3	29	12	11
O-4+	44	7	9

SOURCES: Response rate and total respondents: DoD, 2013, pp. 21–23. Population rate: Office of the Deputy Under Secretary of Defense for Military Community and Family Policy, 2012, p. 15.
NOTE: N = 11,574. The Air Force does not have warrant officers, so that row does not appear in this table.

Overall, the strategy of mailing notices through the post office to personnel without email addresses on file and supplementing the original sample with an additional sample pulled from the same categories as the low responders appears to have been successful in increasing the number of lower-ranking enlisted members in the total sample. We do still observe the pattern of junior officers and junior enlisted members responding at lower rates than NCOs and higher-ranking officers. The study reported that junior enlisted males in particular had low response rates and noted that this military population is "less likely to have regular access to computers and their email accounts depending on their current duty assignment or military occupational specialty" (DoD, 2013, p. 29). Subsequently, the authors recommended that the survey results be interpreted with some caution because those with less access could differ from those with greater access on key measures in the health-related survey; they further recommended that future surveys incorporate a strategy for improving response rates in this group (DoD, 2013, p. 29).

Center for Army Leadership Annual Survey of Army Leadership, 2011

The Center for Army Leadership Annual Survey of Army Leadership is an annual survey examining Army leader attitudes about leadership development, leadership quality, and leadership contributions, which senior decisionmakers can use in developing policy (Riley et al., 2012). The sample focused on active-duty, reserve, and guard NCOs, warrant officers, and officers at or below the rank of colonel.[5] The survey was administered online at the end of 2011 and was approximately 15 minutes long. Although the survey does not include junior enlisted personnel, it does offer the opportunity to examine whether this Army effort also found that those further down the military hierarchy are less likely than higher-ranking members to participate in military-sponsored surveys.

The overall survey response rate for uniformed personnel was 16 percent. Table 2.12 presents each rank group's response rates, composition of the total military survey respondents, population rate for the entire Army, and the percentage of each rank group for just the population of Army leaders (pay grades E-5 to O-10). Once again, response rates were lower among younger, lower-ranking NCOs and officers than among their higher-ranking counterparts. The lowest active-duty response rate, 13 percent, came from junior NCOs, who make up approximately half of Army leadership and 26 percent of all soldiers. Similarly, the lowest response rates for the Army National Guard and Army Reserve (10 percent) were among junior NCOs, who make up 28 percent of all soldiers and 54 percent of leaders in the reserve component.

---

[5] Army civilian leaders are also included in the survey but are out of the scope of this report. Soldiers in pay grades E-1 through E-4 were not included in this survey of leaders only.

Table 2.12 Response Rates by Rank Group for the 2011 Center for Army Leadership Annual Survey of Army Leadership Survey

	Active Duty			Guard and Reserve		
Rank Group	Response Rate (%)	Percentage of Total Respondents	Percentage of Total Population (Leadership Only)	Response Rate (%)	Percentage of Total Respondents	Percentage of Total Population (Leadership Only)
E-5 to E-6	13	29	26 (49)	10	25	28 (54)
E-7 to E-9	21	19	10 (19)	21	22	10 (19)
W-1 to W-5	18	9	3 (5)	19	10	2 (4)
O-1 to O-3	15	26	9 (16)	13	26	6 (13)
O-4 to O-6	28	18	6 (11)	23	18	4 (9)

SOURCES: Response rate and total respondents: Riley et al., 2012, p. 2. Population rate: Office of the Deputy Under Secretary of Defense for Military Community and Family Policy, 2012, pp. 15, 60.
NOTE: N = 16,813.

Conclusion

A survey with a purely random survey sample and in which different subgroups of invitees are equally likely to have the opportunity and motivation to participate should reflect the corresponding population rates. In the military, that means a greater prevalence of younger than older respondents and a greater prevalence of junior- than senior-ranking personnel. A basic-level descriptive analysis of seven large web-based surveys of military personnel showed disproportionately low response rates among one or more of the younger or lower-ranking airman or service member cohorts. No reviewed survey was excluded from this report because this pattern was missing from its response rates.

Other published research suggests that lower response rates among younger military personnel are not confined to online surveys or surveys sponsored by DoD. For example, one 2007–2008 telephone survey of Iraq and Afghanistan war veterans that was not sponsored by DoD found that younger veterans were underrepresented relative to their numbers in the targeted population of veterans (Tanielian and Jaycox, 2008, p. 94). A 2009 survey mailed to U.S. Iraq and Afghanistan war veterans that also offered an opportunity to complete the survey online found that veterans ages 24 to 34 were much less likely to participate than veterans in older age groups (Coughlin et al., 2011). As another example, a postdeployment study of Army National Guard soldiers in four states was conducted online and in person by scholars who are Air Force civilians. They reported an average survey respondent age of 34.50 years (Scott et al., 2011, p. 279), which was higher than the average age of Army National Guard soldiers nationally (30.6 years) (DMDC, 2012b, p. 85). More striking is that no one under the rank of E-6 volunteered at the end of the survey for a follow-on, in-depth interview, so the authors were unable to explore more fully the views of young, enlisted soldiers (Scott et al., 2011, p. 291).

The results presented in this chapter suggest that an overrepresentation of older respondents and underrepresentation of younger respondents is not uncommon in web-based surveys of military personnel, despite variations in research topics, sponsors, recruitment techniques, and other methodological characteristics.

Chapter Three. Low Response Rates in Survey Research and Their Implications

This chapter provides the nonscientific reader an overview of survey researchers' observations of declining survey response rates and hypotheses and investigations into reasons for nonresponse. It explains that high response rates are not necessarily indicative of bias-free results and that, sometimes, low response rates produce the same results as higher response rates without the costs of pursuing nonrespondents. Methods of testing for and addressing nonresponse bias are described.

As U.S. Population Response Rates Decline, Recruitment Efforts Expand

A 2013 report by a panel of experts brought together under the National Research Council's (NRC's) Committee on National Statistics cites overwhelming evidence that survey response rates have significantly declined in the past two decades. For example, the Council of American Survey Research Organizations conducts an annual immunization survey with approximately 35,000 eligible respondents. From 1995 to 2010, response rates plummeted from 87 to 63 percent (NRC, 2013). A similarly large survey by the National Center for Health Statistics known as the National Health Interview Survey has seen responses drop from 80 to 66 percent between 1997 and 2011 (NRC, 2013). Such trends have been observed not just in the United States but also internationally (Groves and Couper, 1998; Stoop et al., 2010) and among both general populations and those in specific organizations (NRC, 2013; Newell, Whittam, et al., 2010).

One meta-analysis found that response rates might be dropping at an even faster pace but that the true decline might be masked as researchers adopt strategies to enhance response rates (Anseel et al., 2010). Surveyors, including the news media and government contract organizations, are fielding surveys for longer periods, increasing call attempts for phone surveys, sending advance notice, offering incentives, and making more attempts to convert refusals into responses. Despite the boost those strategies provide, response rates still have declined significantly over time (Holbrook, Krosnick, and Pfent, 2008; NRC, 2013). The challenge is even greater for web survey modes, whose response rates are reported by meta-analyses to be 11 percent to 14 percent lower than traditional telephone and mailed survey modes (Lozar Manfreda et al., 2008; Shih and Fan, 2008). Overall, the additional strategies have raised survey costs, with the scale depending on such factors as sample sizes, strategies used, and survey modes (NRC, 2013).

Historically, a variety of studies using face-to-face and telephone interviews have found that older people were more likely to respond than younger ones (Campanelli and O'Muircheartaigh,

1999; Hox and de Leeuw, 2002; Singer, Frankel, and Glassman, 1983). One journal article published by Nielsen Company researchers refers to 18- to 34-year-olds as a hard-to-reach subgroup and notes that, given a choice of survey response modes, 74 percent of participants in this age group returned their surveys by mail, 24 percent through the web, and 2 percent by telephone (Burks, Walton, and Bristol, 2014). Other comparative studies of college populations find response rates higher for web than mail surveys, which contrasts with studies of other populations that find responses lower for web than mail surveys (Shih and Fan, 2008). In one 2008–2009 web-based Navy survey of active-duty members, weighted response rates were lower among those ages 27 and under (21 percent) than those ages 28 to 43 (32 percent) and ages 44 and above (44 percent) (Uriell and Clewis, 2012). The youngest group of respondents to this survey, however, was most likely to participate in a concurrent "lightning poll" consisting of five questions sent by text message to their personal cell phones.

Overall, we found it difficult, however, to identify recent methodological studies focusing on young adults' response rates to online surveys. The challenge persisted despite our use of a wide range of standard academic literature review strategies. Our search included soliciting recommendations from survey research experts; reviewing the content and bibliographies of books and articles on survey research methods; and searching the websites of professional survey research journals and organizations, such as *Public Opinion Quarterly*, *Survey Practice*, and the Pew Research Center. We also searched publication databases, such as JSTOR and Google Scholar, using search terms to capture the methodological aspect (e.g., *online*, *web*, *electronic*, or *Internet* combined with *survey*, *poll*, *response rate*, or *nonresponse bias*) and the population (e.g., *age*, *youth*, *young adult*, *generation*, *college*, *military*, or *millennial*) or the names of authors known for publishing in this field (e.g., *Don Dillman* or *Robert Groves*).

We did find some indication, however, that lower online survey response rates among young American adults are not limited to the military population. For example, since 2004, the EDUCAUSE Center for Analysis and Research has conducted an annual survey of undergraduate students in U.S.-based colleges and universities about information technology. The overall response rate to the emailed survey invitation for the online survey—despite drawings for $50 and $100 gift certificates—was 7 percent in 2013 and 9 percent in 2012 (Dahlstrom, Walker, and Dziuban, 2013, p. 43; Dahlstrom, 2012, p. 33). Regarding web-based surveys, Kelton Global, a research consulting firm, states that, although younger adults are generally more comfortable in the digital space than older cohorts, that factor has not translated to higher online survey completion rates (Kelton Global, 2013, p. 9).

What Are Some of the Reasons for Nonresponse?

The National Research Council's assembled panel of experts concluded that "response rates continue on a long-term downward path, but we are concerned that solid evidence about the *reasons* for the decline is still elusive" (NRC, 2013, p. 14). The council's panel recommended more research to identify individual and societal factors responsible for the change, as well as more research on why people choose to participate. This section provides a brief overview of scholarship on reasons for nonresponse.

Lack of Time or Interest

Survey comparisons and follow-up assessments with nonrespondents have identified numerous explanatory factors. Lack of time is one of the primary reasons given for nonresponsiveness in both general (NRC, 2013; Edwards et al., 2009) and military (Newell, Rosenfeld, et al., 2004) populations. Additional factors include lack of incentive, lack of information about or belief in the potential impact of survey responses, lack of topical interest, apathy toward surveys in general, and survey fatigue (Edwards et al., 2009; Newell, Rosenfeld, et al., 2004; Sheehan, 2001). Kelton Global suggests that millennial-generation characteristics, such as being indecisive, overscheduled, and having expectations of a rich, seamless experience across media platforms (e.g., gaming elements, meaningful visuals, and instant gratification), can lead to disengaged survey participation and breakoff (Kelton Global, 2013).[1]

Attitudes Toward Sponsoring Organizations

Research has also suggested that attitudes toward an organization can affect willingness to participate in surveys sponsored by that organization. The national decline in survey participation might in part be related to proliferation of research surveys, marketing surveys, political polls, and unsolicited calls and emails to sell products and services (Galea and Tracy, 2007). Surveys sponsored by commercial enterprises have lower response rates than those sponsored by academic institutions or governmental agencies (Fan and Yan, 2010).

One university-sponsored study attempted to assess the role of attitudes using a survey follow-up design. First, it surveyed students while they were in class and achieved a near-100-percent participation rate. It then followed up several weeks later with an email request, again on behalf of the university, to participate in an online web survey with the chance to win $200 in a raffle. The authors found that, given their responses to the first survey, students who did not participate in the second survey were more likely than their peers to perceive the university as having unfair decisionmaking processes. Nonrespondents were also less likely to believe that the university valued their contributions, cared about their well-being, or had a favorable social exchange relationship with them (Spitzmüller et al., 2006). The implication is that people are less willing to "help out" an organization by completing voluntary surveys when they do not believe that the organization has sufficient regard for their welfare.

---

[1] Americans born between approximately 1982 and 2005 have been labeled the millennial generation (Howe and Strauss, 2007).

Another study using a similar study design found that nursing students registering greater perceptions of "too many job demands and too little time" on an in-person survey were less likely than other nursing students to respond to an email invitation to participate in an online organizational survey (Barr, Spitzmüller, and Stuebing, 2008). The authors posited that this increased sense of overload might contribute to survey nonresponse not only in terms of time available to participate in a survey but also potentially as a sign of resentment for the workload.

In the military context, previous studies have found nonresponse to be driven by such factors as lack of Internet access because of deployment (Newell, Whittam, et al., 2010), lack of endorsements by organizational leaders (Jones et al., 2007), satisfaction with the status quo with respect to the survey aims (Thompson and Surface, 2007), disbelief that the study will have the desired impact (Newell, Whittam, et al., 2010), and topic sensitivity (Olmsted and Whittam, 2004).

It is also possible that lower response rates reflect, in part, some leaders discouraging participation. The lead author of this report has encountered examples of leaders explicitly telling members of their units not to participate in a survey sponsored by that service's headquarters, military personnel complaining of leaders who scold them when unit assessments come back unfavorable, and perceptions of leaders retaliating against people who they believed entered negative comments on a unit survey. These might be rare events, or they might reflect pockets of behavior that undermine senior military leaders' efforts to solicit representative feedback from the force. We are unaware of systematic data that would illuminate the extent to which such behavior might actually occur.

Survey Breakoff

Nonresponse includes not just complete lack of response but also partial completions, or survey breakoff. Response rates typically count only completed or mostly completed surveys as a response. People who might have begun the survey but quit early are said to have broken off and are counted as nonrespondents. Thus, survey length might contribute to nonresponse bias by discouraging both initiation of a survey and its completion.

Internet surveys tend to have high rates of breakoff (Peytchev, 2009). In the case of junior enlisted military personnel, they might be as likely to start the survey as other subgroups but less likely to complete it. The literature provides evidence that education and youth—potentially indicators of cognitive sophistication—can explain breakoff in online health surveys, particularly when the questions are long or judgment-intensive and when many questions appear on each survey page (Peytchev, 2009). Young people are also more likely to access online surveys using smartphones, which is also associated with higher breakoff rates (Lambert and Miller, 2015).

Survey analysts choose how to define *survey breakoff* and *survey completion*. For example, DoD surveys often count a survey with about 50 percent or more of the items completed as a completed survey (e.g., DMDC, 2012c, 2012d, 2012e, 2012f). Survey response rates would change and survey weights might change if more or less of the survey needed to be completed to meet the definition of *complete*. The RAND 2012 survey described in Chapter One required that a respondent reach the end of the survey (whether he or she volunteered a response to the final questions or not) for that survey to be considered complete and included in the response rate calculations and analytic data set. If the demographics of those who reach the end of the survey differ from those who complete only half of it, the reported response rates and the survey weights in some DoD surveys could mask nonresponse biases for items at the end of the survey.

Internet-Related Barriers to Participation

In web-based and email surveys, technology and its access can play a substantial role in responsiveness in terms of whether an invitation is received, completed, and returned (Dillman, Smyth, and Christian, 2009; Fan and Yan, 2010; Newell, Whittam, et al., 2010; Thompson and Surface, 2007). In military populations, these factors could be related to age if younger and older service members have differential computer access (Newell, Whittam, et al., 2010). Indeed, according to a report on survey completion in the U.S. Navy, commissioned officers report slightly more email and Internet access than enlisted sailors (Olmsted and Whittam, 2004), although that might no longer be true given ship upgrades in the past decade. Some service members might have computer access at work but only very limited access and competing requirements for the time they do have available, such as computer-based training.

Some challenges related to soliciting participation and conducting a survey through the Internet are connected with issues of trust. Perceptions of privacy and anonymity in the survey process can also be a hurdle (Thompson et al., 2003). People might feel greater security in mailing in a paper survey with checked boxes than completing a survey online using a work or personal computer or mobile device. Online survey research has been hampered by the consequences of increasingly widespread distrust of electronic communications spurred by fears of online scams, identity theft, computer viruses, and the like (Dillman, Smyth, and Christian, 2009). Spam filters and junk-mail settings might keep survey invitations from ever reaching their intended recipients. Military personnel receive training and reminders that warn them to protect against potential cyber threats. Moreover, the Pew Research Center has found that the generation of millennial American adults, now ranging in age from 18 to 33, are much less trusting of others than adults in older generations (19 percent of millennials say that, "generally speaking, most people can be trusted," compared with 31 percent or higher for the earlier generations [Pew Research Center, 2014, p. 7]).

Strategies to Reduce Nonresponse in the 2012 RAND Information and Communication Technology and Well-Being Survey

The RAND team took many steps to promote participation in the 2012 ICT and well-being survey, based on concerns and advice commonly documented in the literature (Dillman, Smyth, and Christian, 2009), but we do not know how they were received or whether they had different levels of influence on different subgroups. Appendix A provides detailed information about the challenges and strategies employed to promote participation in the 2012 RAND survey of airmen on ICT and well-being. Appendix B presents the template for the invitation for that survey, which reflects some of these strategies.

A brief version of the details presented in those appendixes reveals possible reasons for nonresponse on that survey. We hoped that the focus on ICTs might interest young adults because that age group in the United States uses most of these technologies at the highest rates (Pew Research Center, 2014). We were aware, however, that airmen might be wary of yet another survey or more official communication addressing mental health. Moreover, policy presents hurdles to offering incentives in human subjects research: We would have had to ensure that survey participation was restricted to nonduty hours or offered an unconditional gift to everyone whether they participated or not. In terms of airmen's time, invitees had months to participate in the survey and were sent regular reminders of its availability, as well as notice of when the survey window was about to close. Still, administration over the summer was not a preferred time because airmen might be moving or on vacation then and reserve-component personnel might not meet during this period. The survey might also have been at a disadvantage in that it was not a familiar, recurring survey with a track record of influencing Air Force decisions, nor did we have local advocates promoting survey participation. Our study methods attempted both to demonstrate that the survey was a legitimate enterprise endorsed by the Air Force and to assure invitees that their individual responses would be protected. We personalized the survey invitations to try to appeal to recipients directly, but the ability to automate personalization today might make that technique less effective than it has been historically.

What Is Considered a Low Response Rate?

High response rates are presumed to be an indicator of quality and lack of bias in surveys, but no minimum response rate has ever been established as a scientific threshold for minimizing nonresponse bias:

> There is no scientifically proven minimally acceptable response rate. A response rate of 60% has been used as the threshold of acceptability by some and has face validity as a measure of survey quality; however, similar to $P < .05$ in statistical comparisons, 60% is only a "rule of thumb" that masks a more complex issue. Empirical assessments over the past decade have concluded that the response rate of a survey may not be as strongly associated with the quality or representativeness of the survey as had been generally believed. This research has led to an increasing recognition that the degree to which sampled respondents differ from the survey population as a whole (i.e., nonresponse bias) is central to evaluating the representativeness of a survey, rather than response rates per se. Indeed, a survey with a relatively high response rate, albeit one in which nonrespondents are very different from respondents, might produce far more biased results than a survey with a lower response rate from a truly random and representative group of respondents. (Johnson and Wislar, 2012, p. 1805)

The Office of Management and Budget (OMB) must review and approve federally sponsored data collection from the public, although voluntary surveys of active-duty and retired service members and their families are excluded. Nevertheless, its standards and guidelines recommend an analysis of nonresponse bias for surveys with a response rate less than 80 percent (OMB, 2006), which is much higher than the response rates in the DoD surveys we reviewed.

Researchers look not just for whether bias exists but also for the magnitude of the bias. With the same response rate, the degree of bias may differ according to the relationship between the characteristics of the underrepresented population and the topics measured on the survey. With some topics, there might be no bias, while other survey results might hide various amounts of nonresponse bias.

Do Low Response Rates Mean That Survey Results Are Biased?

Low response rates alone do not equal a biased survey sample: Nonresponse bias occurs only when those who did not respond to the survey would have answered the questions differently from those who did. If only 30 percent of a population responds to a survey, but the other 70 percent would respond the same way, then a nonresponse bias would not be present.

As nonresponse to household surveys has grown, so too have the costs of administering those surveys because of the pursuit of high response rates (Groves, 2006). Striving for high response rates has been and can be an effective way to attempt to reduce nonresponse bias. But as noted earlier, all too often, people assume that high response rates produce information that is more complete and less biased or unbiased. However, scholars have demonstrated that high response rates can still contain response bias, and some studies find the same results when both low and high response rates are compared. A meta-analysis of 30 survey methodological studies reported that, in "the linkage between nonresponse rates and nonresponse biases, we find large nonresponse biases for some statistics but no strong empirical relationship between response rates and nonresponse bias" (Groves, 2006, p. 663). A subsequent meta-analysis of 59 studies designed to estimate correlates of nonresponse concluded that, when the reasons for participation are highly correlated with the survey measures, large nonresponse biases can occur and high response rates are less likely to reduce the odds of nonresponse bias (Groves and Peytcheva, 2008). Those same observations might or might not hold for DoD populations or the topics assessed on its surveys.

DMDC ascertained that, if a nonresponse bias exists in its SOFSs, it is not due to online administration as opposed to a mailed survey. It also determined that the costs of producing, mailing, receiving, and scanning paper surveys might increase the response rates but do not otherwise produce a significant difference in the results:

> Beginning with the first test of the SOFS in 2002, DMDC has periodically included tests of methodology differences affecting response rates and data quality. Such tests have concluded that a follow-up paper survey increases response rates by around seven percentage points without significantly or

> meaningfully changing estimates from the survey. (U.S. Government Accountability Office [GAO], 2010, p. 6)

Comparative studies of telephone surveys have found similar results. A study of a national random-digit-dialing telephone survey compared responses from two modes of administration:

- One was open for five days with a minimum of ten attempts to reach someone at each number and usually at least one attempt to convert a refusal.
- The other was open for more than 21 weeks and involved sending advance letters (some with $2 incentives), sending letters attempting to convert refusals, and leaving voice-mail messages.

The survey effort that made more-rigorous attempts to solicit participation obtained twice the response rate of the five-day survey (50 percent versus 25 percent) (Keeter et al., 2006, p. 763). However, for 77 of 84 comparable survey items, the samples were statistically indistinguishable (Keeter et al., 2006, p. 759).

In another example, a study examined three telephone health surveys on the topics of mental health and substance abuse and health-care insurance and access. The purpose was to discern whether the surveys' results might have been different if less aggressive strategies for reaching respondents had been used (Davern et al., 2010). The surveys made nine or more attempts to contact each household and some attempts to convert refusals, but a less aggressive strategy (only one to four attempts to contact and no attempts at converting refusals) would have

- produced lower response rates (26 percent to 37 percent, compared with 45 percent to 59 percent)
- cost less than half as much to administer
- obtained essentially the same survey results.

The authors concluded that, "for some studies, money spent on aggressively pursuing high response rates could be better used to increase statistical power and/or to directly examine nonresponse bias" (Davern et al., 2010, p. 1324). Because evidence questioning the added value of higher response rates relative to the costs of acquiring them has grown, the National Research Council has recommended more research to empirically establish these trade-offs (NRC, 2013).

A final example is older but still relevant and perhaps unique. For an entire year in the mid-1990s, during the first week of basic military training, every Air Force recruit completed a behavioral risk questionnaire on such topics as smoking, alcohol use, diet, and physical activity (Klesges et al., 1999). The last question asked recruits to imagine being called at home and being asked to participate in some important research: Would they participate? Recruits could then be categorized into those who said no, those who said yes, and those who said yes but depending on the circumstances. Analyses revealed that recruits who said they definitely would not participate in the phone survey (20 percent) were more likely than their peers to report engaging in unhealthy lifestyles. However, when the researchers compared the results for 100 percent of the recruit population to the results for the 80 percent who would or would likely participate in the phone survey, the overall survey differences were consistently less than 1 percentage point

(Klesges et al., 1999, p. 1230). In other words, even seemingly large differences between groups and their response rates might not necessarily bear on the particular study results.

The purpose of this section is not to suggest that nonresponse bias does not exist or that response rates are unimportant but to illustrate that lower response rates can sometimes produce the same results on a given set of topics as higher response rates that are more costly to administer, and so such considerations must be made on a case-by-case basis.

How Can We Address Nonresponse Bias?

One way analysts think about nonresponse is as a problem of missing data. When people do not participate in a survey, their survey responses are missing. Ideally, their responses are missing completely at random, meaning that the overall survey results would be the same with or without the missing data, regardless of whether the pattern itself is random. If they are missing at random, then some people are disproportionately likely to respond, but the missing responses are associated with characteristics that can be acquired from other sources for both participants and nonparticipants (such as data on gender, age, or pay grade contained in personnel files). The reason this is preferable is that the data can be adjusted (weighted) to proportions that would correct for the bias.[2] However, the factors that influence survey responses might not be recorded in any available data sets. It is important to learn what influences the likelihood of responding so we can properly weight the data and caveat the survey results. An auxiliary effort paired with a survey effort would be needed to explore whether any nonresponse bias is associated with the outcomes being measured. Regardless of whether a supplementary study is conducted, efforts to increase response rates should focus on ways to reduce the missing data that account for the nonresponse bias (not just hit a target overall response rate). In other words, efforts to increase response rates should consider whose views might be underrepresented and specifically target the barriers those populations could be facing.

Compare Characteristics of Respondents and Nonrespondents and Correct for Differences

The primary way in which DoD-sponsored surveys can and usually do attempt to address nonresponse bias is to look at demographic data on military personnel and weight the survey sample so it corresponds proportionately to the key demographics. This correction is often standard, using characteristics that are either logical to include or have proven relevant in past studies (e.g., gender, service, service component, marital status, race and ethnicity, age, or rank group). For example, if gender is associated with attitudes toward opening combat arms occupations to military women, and military men are significantly less likely than military

[2] For a more detailed and technical discussion of missing data, see Little and Rubin, 2002.

women to respond to the survey, then the unweighted survey results could reflect a nonresponse bias. Survey researchers correct for this type of problem by weighting the survey responses so they are proportionate to the gender ratio in the military population. If responses to survey items do not vary significantly by a characteristic, then weighting the sample to reflect the composition of the force along that characteristic is unnecessary because it will not change the results.

DMDC explains that the extensive data available on military populations provide great opportunities for assessing and correcting for potential bias caused by differing response rates across subgroups:

> DMDC statisticians assert that SOFS surveys likely have lower levels of nonresponse bias than surveys with much higher response rates because generally survey organizations know very little about survey nonrespondents, and consequently have limited accessible data to assist with nonresponse adjustments.
> . . .
>
> DMDC has an uncommon and advantageous position as a surveyor by maintaining extremely detailed, complete, and timely administrative data for our entire survey frames. Due to this complete sampling frame, DMDC has more extensive information regarding the characteristics of survey nonrespondents prior to conducting nonresponse analysis studies than most other survey organizations know after such studies. For the SOFS program, DMDC uses this thorough knowledge of nonrespondents both for statistical imputations for item-missing data and nonresponse and post-stratification weighting adjustments to compensate for unit nonresponse. Both of these procedures are specifically designed to reduce nonresponse bias in [SOFS] estimates. (GAO, 2010, p. 6)

Thus, for DoD, the challenge might be narrowed down to detecting relevant population differences that do not break along demographic boundaries, such as variation by preferences, attitudes, experiences, health, or other characteristics not easily accessible or not captured in military personnel administrative databases.

Find Out More About the Views of Nonrespondents to Appropriately Caveat Survey Results

OMB guidelines for federally sponsored voluntary surveys of nonmilitary populations recommend an analysis of nonresponse bias for surveys with a response rate of less than 80 percent (OMB, 2006).

GAO recommended that DMDC follow up on its surveys more frequently to investigate nonresponse:

> While we acknowledge that DMDC takes some steps to address nonresponse—for example, monitoring response rates for a fixed set of variables and incorporating statistical weighting techniques in its survey estimates—monitoring response rates without performing more in-depth nonresponse analysis may not necessarily identify problems with nonresponse bias. (GAO, 2010, p. 4)

DMDC concurred with GAO's recommendation and does conduct some follow-up analyses (e.g., DMDC, 2014).

If the bias in the survey responses rests in the difference between those who participate in the survey and those who do not, then after-the-fact knowledge about how those nonrespondents differ can help inform the appropriate caveats for interpreting the results. For example, one might find that respondents to a survey about a policy debate are more likely to feel strongly about the issue on either end of the spectrum, and nonrespondents are disinterested in the issue and would be satisfied with whatever direction that policy reform took. In that case, regardless of whether the response rate was 30 percent or 60 percent, a nonresponse bias would still exist. The survey results could be qualified as overestimating the strength of the population's opinions. Alternatively, it might be the case that people opposed to the status quo were more motivated to participate to register their desire for change; then a different caveat would accompany the survey results.

Surveys on mental health–related topics might find that the nonresponse bias is related to people who are depressed being less likely to participate because they are less motivated to participate in things in general, and thus self-rated population measures of mental health are overly positive. On the other hand, depressed people might find a mental health–related survey directly relevant to them and be more likely than nondepressed people to participate. Or it could be that both occur at similar rates and cancel each other out. An exploration of nonresponse bias can shed light on this concern.

Survey researchers have developed a variety of methods for investigating the presence and nature of survey nonresponse bias (Andridge and Little, 2011; Groves, 2006). One way to test for nonresponse bias is to follow up with a sample of nonrespondents shortly after a survey has closed and attempt to conduct interviews, including asking a sample of the key survey items. Those responses can be compared with the responses of those who participated in the survey and then tested for statistically significant differences. Postsurvey interviews could also pursue reasons for lack of participation to identify any hurdles that could be addressed in future surveys.

Another approach that survey researchers use to explore potential nonbias in a survey is to compare those who are early responders to a survey invitation with those who are later responders. The hypothesis is that late responders might be similar to those who did not respond and thus might suggest the attitudes of those who did not participate in the survey. DMDC's assessment of nonresponse bias in the 2012 Workplace and Gender Relations Survey of Active Duty Members included just such an analysis (DMDC, 2014). DMDC found a variety of demographic differences according to timing of the responses, but the most pronounced was by pay grade: Thirty-five percent of early responders, 46 percent of late responders, and 67 percent of nonrespondents were E-1 to E-4s (DMDC, 2014, p. 40). However, after analyzing the responses to the questions on unwanted sexual contact, DMDC concluded that, if the late responders are indeed suggestive of the missing data from the nonrespondents, then there is little evidence of nonresponse bias in that survey.

Address Barriers to Survey Response for Those with Underrepresented Views

If the goal is to reduce nonresponse bias, and not just to capture more of the same types of participants for the appearance of higher response rates, then recruitment strategies need to focus on participants whose experiences and opinions are underrepresented. Thus, the previous steps of identifying whether nonresponse bias exists and, if they do, the reasons for nonresponse, are important prerequisites to developing strategies to recruit a more representative sample. Without that knowledge, additional time, effort, and expense might be wasted just to end up with the same survey findings.

If service members experiencing job overload are less likely than other members to respond to military surveys, then such surveys could underestimate the degree of stress on the force and potentially associated factors, such as reenlistment intentions or indicators of service member and family well-being. Strategies to address this survey hurdle would need to focus on unit leaders making time available for even overworked people to stop and take a 15- to 20-minute survey. Such efforts would also communicate the importance that leadership places on receiving feedback from that population through the survey vehicle.

Announcements about survey results and subsequent leadership actions can convey the value of participation to those who doubt that surveys matter. However, if these news items focus only on the positive results or views of the numerical majority, they could alienate service members holding dissenting views, creating or contributing to nonresponse bias in future surveys. If military leaders demonstrate that they hear and value less common perspectives as well and are at least working to address the negative feedback even if they do not have an immediate solution, they could help prevent or reduce this type of nonresponse bias.

Conclusion

Response rates have declined significantly in the past two decades. The reasons for survey nonresponse can be difficult to ascertain. However, some follow-up assessments have identified several factors, including perceived lack of time, survey length, lack of incentive, lack of feedback about findings and impact, lack of topical interest, survey fatigue, computer access problems, junk-mail settings, and perceptions of privacy and anonymity. Other research suggests that a respondent is less likely to respond to a survey if he or she has a negative attitude toward the survey's sponsor. The literature also provides evidence that education and youth can be a factor in respondents not completing a survey when the questions are long or judgment-intensive or when multiple questions are included on a survey page.

Meanwhile, an effort to bolster response rates might actually mask the degree to which willingness to participate has declined over time. Surveyors are giving respondents longer to answer, increasing call attempts for phone surveys, sending advance notice, offering incentives, and making more effort to convert refusals into responses. This extra effort, of course, results in additional costs.

Are these attempts at increasing response rates worth the effort? The research suggests that, in some cases, they might not be. Higher response rates are thought to protect against nonresponse bias—that is, the degree to which respondents differ from the survey population as a whole. But this bias occurs only when those who did not respond to a survey would have answered the questions differently from those who did respond. Scholars have demonstrated that high response rates can still yield data that have response bias, and some studies find the same results when low and high response rates are compared. As evidence questioning the added value of higher response rates relative to the costs of acquiring them has grown, the National Research Council has recommended more research to empirically establish these trade-offs.

Several ways to address nonresponse bias do not involve such costly and herculean efforts to increase the response rate:

- Compare characteristics of respondents and nonrespondents and correct for differences.
- Find out more about the views of nonrespondents to appropriately caveat survey results.
- Address barriers to survey access for underrepresented groups whose characteristics might be correlated with the survey topics.

Chapter Four. Conclusion and Recommendations for Future Air Force and Other Military Surveys

Responses to the RAND Survey as the Basis for Further Exploration

The RAND team employed a variety of strategies to enhance response rates among airmen in the 2012 RAND ICT and well-being survey conducted for the AF/SG. Some known and possibly unknown challenges to response rates remained. Ultimately, response rates among 18- to 24-year-old airmen were lower than for the other age groups and lower among junior enlisted airmen than airmen of other ranks. The team included only surveys in which respondents had reached the end. Partial surveys that were excluded were more likely to have come from active-duty airmen, junior enlisted personnel, and 18- to 24-year-olds than their counterparts. Because all responses were anonymous and not linkable to individual identities, we cannot discern whether that pattern represents higher rates of disruption during the survey (and thus airmen returning and starting the survey again) or whether it represents higher rates of dropping out of the survey entirely.

This rank discrepancy for completed surveys might be a function of age differences: The AFPC IDEAS demographic database shows that (as of September 2012) 96 percent of active-duty airmen at the entry-level enlisted rank (E-1) were 24 or younger, compared with 69 percent of active-duty airmen at the entry-level officer rank (O-1) who were that young. Because a college degree is a prerequisite for an officer commission but not for enlistment, this difference is not surprising.

Lower response rates among junior enlisted airmen might also be a function of officer and enlisted disparities: Enlisted personnel might have limited time or less access to the Internet, be less willing to participate as a result of less positive views of the organization, or have less interest in the survey topic. Other factors might be at play as well.

As with most survey research, the 2012 RAND survey did not attempt to determine whether lower response rates introduced a nonresponse bias. As a result, we do not know whether those who did not participate in the survey would have responded significantly differently from those who did participate, so we do not know whether a higher response rate would have produced different results. Because of Air Force demographic data, the RAND study was able to employ one standard method for addressing nonresponse, weighting the data to correspond to several key variables (age group; officer/enlisted status; gender; and active-duty, guard, or reserve status).

The Low Response Pattern Appears Across U.S. Department of Defense Surveys

A brief review of available information on seven large, recurring web-based surveys of military personnel sponsored by several DoD organizations suggests that these efforts also face challenges recruiting participants in the younger age groups or junior ranks. Lower response rates for these subgroups appear across surveys despite differences in survey topics, survey sponsors, sampling strategies, recruitment methods, and survey administration. Surveys in the U.S. population more broadly have also reported lower response rates among younger adults, including college students, although the body of research focusing on this topic for web surveys is limited.

Low Response Does Not Necessarily Yield Biased Results

What do these lower response rates mean? No minimum response rate has been established in the survey research community as necessary for valid results. Researchers commonly aim to reduce the risk of nonresponse bias by working to increase response rates, but higher response rates do not rule out nonresponse bias. Extra recruiting measures might succeed only in engaging more participants with similar experiences and views. As more research has been conducted to test for nonresponse bias, more studies have found similar or statistically identical findings between surveys with higher and lower response rates. Additionally, scholars caution that certain recruiting strategies could introduce or increase nonresponse bias by appealing to subpopulations with particular motives. For example, if lower response rates are due to access issues, additional reminders might succeed in recruiting more members who regularly work on computers with Internet access and skew the results in the direction of office workers, supervisors, and managers. Or those motivated to participate because of financial incentives might hold different views or come from different backgrounds from those motivated to participate for altruistic reasons.

Recommendations

The Air Force should consider the recommendations provided in this section so it can better understand and address nonresponse in its surveys. Our first recommendations for further research are in line with GAO recommendations for DoD and with recommendations by the National Research Council for survey research more broadly, and thus could apply to other military surveys as well.

Explore Reasons Behind Nonresponse

Is nonresponse related to access, work overload, survey features, topic interest, attitudes toward the organization, attitudes toward surveys in general, privacy concerns, or other issues?

This question can be explored both systematically and scientifically through research, but requests for feedback could also be conducted less formally through town-hall meetings, in which senior leaders (such as major-command leaders) meet with junior enlisted and junior officer airmen without other members of their chains of command present.

Examine Whether Nonresponse Among Younger Airmen Reflects Lower Rates of Beginning Surveys or Lower Rates of Completing Surveys

Survey breakoff among younger or lower-ranking airmen could result from the survey length, item complexity, subject matter, or judgment-intensive items rather than lesser access to the Internet or initial unwillingness to participate in a survey. If younger or enlisted airmen are more likely to drop out mid-survey, the Air Force could conduct sensitivity analyses to determine whether decisions about how to define surveys as completed (e.g., 50 percent of items or more) and how to construct the survey weights have an impact on the outcomes of interest. It could also consider placing items believed to be related to age and officer/enlisted status at the front of the survey.

Consider Additional Strategies to Increase Response Rates That Could Benefit the Air Force in Other Ways

The Air Force is already attempting to reduce the number of surveys it administers and limit overlap. Additional strategies to increase response rates might be worth the investment if they would provide value in other ways as well. For example, ensuring that all airmen have routine access at work to their Air Force email accounts could not only increase their opportunities to participate in surveys; it could also increase their opportunities to access important information provided by Air Force leadership and health professionals. Also, efforts to fill in missing contact information or correct erroneous addresses for airmen in the Air Force personnel data files could have similar benefits beyond addressing survey response rates.

Relatively low-cost approaches to increasing response rates and reducing data missingness might be worthwhile as strategies that could be employed in the near term, but we caution leaders that an increase in response rates does not necessarily mean that the results are representative. The survey sponsors could tailor recruitment emails to send to a random sample of junior officers and junior enlisted and have the survey analysts use scientific methods to detect whether targeted appeals increase response rates, relative to those of junior officers and junior enlisted personnel who do not receive targeted appeals. Language along the following lines might be appropriate for an Air Force survey:

> In recent years, leadership has noticed lower participation rates among young officer and young enlisted Airmen. You represent the future of the Air Force, and Air Force senior leaders want to make sure they have some insight into your experiences and opinions. Although senior leaders interact with young Airmen face to face, confidential surveys like these help them place those views into context. This is a voluntary survey: As you make your decision, we ask you to

> consider contributing to your Air Force in this way and encouraging your peers to participate as well so that the voices of young Airmen can be counted along with those of NCOs and more-senior officers.

If young airmen are less likely to receive these invitations or read them, the language might make no difference in response rates. Similarly, it might not influence those who are cynical about or alienated from the organization and might not take the message as genuine. But it is a relatively low-cost approach to try.

Do Not Invest Significant Resources in Efforts Solely to Increase Response Rates Across Air Force Surveys Without First Testing Whether There Is Any Value in Doing So

Response rates are not a sufficient metric for concluding whether the survey results are representative of the views of the population. Demographic data can provide clues to the potential for bias and help to correct for it, but other factors not recorded in personnel databases might influence the decision or ability to participate in a survey.

Conduct Further Research to Test for Nonresponse Bias in Online Surveys

With strategies developed by survey researchers, analysts should assess whether lower response rates among the younger, junior officer, and junior enlisted personnel on major Air Force surveys result in nonresponse bias or low representation of those subgroups, despite weighting responses to make them demographically proportionate to the Air Force.

It can experiment with sending paper surveys as follow-ups to nonrespondents, then analyze whether the responses of those who reply by mail differ significantly from responses from those who answered online. Questions added to the end of the paper survey could assess whether Internet access, privacy issues, or other reasons explain nonresponse, which could inform future efforts to reduce barriers to participation (e.g., increasing computer availability to certain populations during Air Force headquarters survey periods).

The Air Force can examine whether those who are last to participate in a survey tend to respond differently from those who respond early on; late responders might offer views somewhat similar to views of those who do not participate at all.

Make Surveys Mobile-Friendly

The Air Force should consider fundamentally changing the way surveys are designed to account for the evolving nature of Internet access. Given the explosion of smartphone and computer tablet use, which is highest among younger adults (Fox and Rainie, 2014), researchers conducting surveys on behalf of DoD should consider designing shorter surveys with those devices in mind. As AAPOR notes, "If you are conducting online surveys, you are conducting mobile surveys" (Link et al., 2014, p. 5).

It is not enough for survey programmers to prepare a mobile-compatible version of a survey designed for computers. Items presented in a grid layout might be easy to scan and complete quickly on a computer, but they can be difficult to navigate on a small screen. Programming the items to appear one by one on a mobile device can dramatically increase the length or at least perceived length of the survey, so survey efforts might need to become even simpler and shorter than researchers already strive to make them (Link et al., 2014). Surveys could focus on fewer, higher-priority topics, or surveys could become more frequent but each much less time-consuming.

The potential value of surveys designed with mobile devices in mind could be tested, particularly to explore whether the design fundamentally changes the populations that participate in Air Force surveys, as well as the findings these efforts obtain. Redesigning surveys for mobile platforms would incur some expense, but it might become the best way to engage future generations in the survey feedback mechanisms for senior military leaders.

Conclusion

Expert advice on strategies to increase survey response rates is readily available (e.g., Dillman, Smyth, and Christian, 2009; Kelton Global, 2013), but the military already uses many of these strategies, and additional efforts might not be warranted. If the armed forces simply adopted new strategies to increase response rates for their online surveys, they could end up doing little more than wasting resources for appearance's sake. Even worse, efforts could introduce or exacerbate existing nonresponse biases. But if age- or rank-related nonresponse biases do exist in Air Force and other military surveys, then additional strategies that target the reasons for nonresponse should be implemented. Research efforts to assess nonresponse bias could simultaneously seek to identify barriers to survey participation and whether these vary by age, rank, or other characteristics.

Some additional strategies to increase response rates might benefit the Air Force in other ways and, for those reasons, could be adopted even without further study. For example, ensuring that all airmen have routine access at work to their Air Force email accounts could not only increase their opportunities to receive survey invitations and participate in surveys requiring CAC access but could also increase their opportunities to access important information provided by Air Force leadership and health professionals. Efforts to fill in missing contact information or correct erroneous addresses for airmen in the Air Force personnel data files could have similar benefits beyond addressing survey response rates.[1]

Before undertaking any extensive efforts focused solely on increasing response rates, however, the military should first seek to determine whether increased response rates would

---

[1] Other factors that can influence response rates are discussed in Appendix A.

result in any fundamentally different outcomes on its key survey items. If the young service members who participate in the surveys generally reflect the range of views held by those who do not participate, then weighting survey responses to reflect the age and rank composition of the population is sufficient to correct for uneven response rates across subgroups. There would be cause for concern, though, if the personnel who do not respond differ in key aspects assessed by the survey items. The overall depiction of military personnel and their needs could be skewed, for example, if those less likely to participate in surveys are more likely to be depressed, in poor physical health, afraid of reprisals over their responses, cynical about service leadership, planning to leave the military, or even satisfied with the status quo.

The Air Force sponsors at least three major Air Force–wide surveys of airmen every two years, with content that includes leadership climate, organizational commitment, Air Force facilities and services, and the health and welfare of airmen and their families. A great deal of time and expense are routinely devoted to developing and administering the surveys and to analyzing, packaging, and reporting the findings. Because the results are used in decisionmaking processes, leaders need to understand how closely those results reflect the attitudes and experiences of all airmen, young and old, and survey participants and nonparticipants alike.

Appendix A. Strategies Used to Promote Participation in the 2012 RAND Survey of Airmen on Information and Communication Technologies and Well-Being

This appendix provides more-detailed descriptions about the survey design, recruitment, and administration features that were intended to promote participation in the RAND 2012 survey of airmen on ICTs and well-being.

Strategies Employed to Promote Participation

Topic and Relevance

Research has shown that survey topic interest can influence survey participation decisions (Groves, Presser, and Dipko, 2004). The opening lines of the 2012 RAND survey invitation explained that it was "a survey to help educate Air Force leadership about the role of the Internet, mobile phones, social media and other technologies in Airmen's lives" (see Appendix B to read the invitation template). We thought that the ICT portion of the research topic might interest airmen, in part because American adults younger than 50 are enthusiastic adopters of technology (see Fox and Rainie, 2014) and in part because it was an uncommon topic in major Air Force and DoD surveys. The survey invitation noted,

> We will also ask you a few questions about your own social interactions and mental health. Additionally, we will ask you about using technologies to access information and support services to enhance the social and mental fitness of yourself and others.

Airmen were also informed that they could answer only the questions they felt comfortable answering and that they could stop taking the survey at any time. To enable airmen to skip mental health–related questions, the survey was programmed so it did not force the respondent to answer questions in order to advance to the next set of questions.[1] A group of airmen who reviewed a full draft of the survey had warned that airmen might be tired of taking mental health–related surveys. However, they also advised that it would be better to mention up front that mental health items were part of the survey than to have airmen later feel "tricked" into another mental health survey.[2]

---

[1] Ultimately, we detected no patterns indicating that airmen who chose to participate were less willing to respond to mental health questions than to any other questions.

[2] For the proper informed consent of participants, we would have revealed this survey focus anyway.

The survey invitation explained how the results could be used and how the subsequent impact could be relevant to airmen. It explained that the survey had "the aim of helping to shape Air Force policy and the way the Air Force uses technology to support the social and mental well-being of Airmen and their families." It also stated, "Your participation is very important and will help ensure that Air Force leadership correctly understands positive and negative aspects of these technologies and takes effective approaches to relevant policy and support service outreach." We had hoped that the potential influence on policy and services, combined with the novel topic of ICT, would encourage participation.

Survey Length

With survey length in mind, we asked the sponsor whether we should conduct a broad assessment of a wide range of topics or an in-depth treatment of just a few topics. The sponsor chose the former, with the intention of using those results to identify any areas that might require more-detailed follow-up. After an initial survey draft was prepared and reviewed, the research team prioritized the drafted survey items and trimmed those less central to the key line of inquiry in order to reduce the expected time for respondents to complete the survey to about 15 to 20 minutes.

Personalized Survey Invitations

Previous research has shown that personalized survey invitations can yield higher response rates than impersonal ones, so this strategy is commonly recommended. However, the value of this in an era of automated invitations has yet to be fully assessed, and it might be less effective when emails are sent to more than one person at a time (Anseel et al., 2010; Dillman, Smyth, and Christian, 2009). The purpose of personalization is to encourage participation by appealing to invitees as people: to draw them out of the group and establish a connection between the respondent and the surveyor (Dillman, Smyth, and Christian, 2009, p. 272). We addressed the invitations to each airman, inserting his or her rank and name at the top of the body of the email, and used individual email addresses recorded in the May 2012 Air Force personnel administrative data files. The email also ended with the name of the project leader.

Information Security

Air Force personnel are trained to maintain online information security, including being wary of unauthorized attempts to access sensitive information or attempts to install malware that might be masked as official requests. The RAND team took several steps to assure recipients that the email invitation and survey were legitimate and authorized by the U.S. Air Force.

To address security concerns about the source of the email invitations, the invitations were digitally signed by a DoD CAC held by the RAND staff sending the invitations. A CAC—DoD's standard identification card for U.S. military personnel, DoD civilian employees, and eligible contractors—is a smart card with embedded electronic data about the cardholder. Using a smart-card reader connected to a computer, the sender can digitally sign an email, verifying to the recipient that the named sender is the actual sender of the message.

As another way to prevent the email invitations from being routed into junk-mail or spam filters, the emails were sent in small batches: 500 at a time, which took about two hours for the software program to digitally sign and send.

The team also provided options that recipients could use to verify the legitimacy of the survey. The invitation included the survey control number issued by the Air Force Survey Office verifying that it had been reviewed and approved, and it provided a link to the Air Force website listing approved surveys. In addition, the invitation offered a separate link to an Air Force website where invitees could view a signed survey support letter on letterhead from the Air Force Deputy Surgeon General. The letter also included commercial and military telephone numbers and an email address for the Air Force colonel from that office who served as the survey point of contact.

Privacy

The steps taken to personalize the invitations and verify their legitimacy could raise airmen's concerns about the privacy afforded survey respondents. Communicating privacy protections was important for several reasons. We wanted to encourage participation in the survey, and we wanted airmen to feel comfortable so they would be open and honest, even on questions they might consider sensitive (e.g., self-rated mental health). Notification that identities and individual responses are protected is also an important component of the informed-consent requirement for research involving human subjects.

The research team wanted to clearly convey that, although the study was being conducted for the Air Force, RAND is an independent organization that is not a part of the military. The survey invitation introduced RAND as a nonprofit, nonpartisan research company. We sent all survey invitations from a rand.org email address, not from a military address identified by the ending .mil. The survey site was hosted on a nonmilitary domain (a rand.org website), as indicated by the web address in the invitation message. The survey invitation explained that the survey could be accessed via computer or smartphone and that the respondent did not have to be on a military network to access it. Thus, in the RAND survey, an airman would not receive the warning message presented when logging into the Air Force military website portal with a CAC that indicates that the U.S. government could access the survey responses (see Figure A.1).

Figure A.1 March 2015 Version of the Notice upon Entering the Air Force Military Website Portal

⚠ NOTICE

YOU ARE ACCESSING A U.S. GOVERNMENT (USG) INFORMATION SYSTEM (IS) THAT IS PROVIDED FOR USG-AUTHORIZED USE ONLY.

By using this IS (which includes any device attached to this IS), you consent to the following conditions:

- The USG routinely intercepts and monitors communications on this IS for purposes including, but not limited to, penetration testing, COMSEC monitoring, network operations and defense, personnel misconduct (PM), law enforcement (LE), and counterintelligence (CI) investigations.
- At any time, the USG may inspect and seize data stored on this IS.
- Communications using, or data stored on, this IS are not private, are subject to routine monitoring, interception, and search, and may be disclosed or used for any USG authorized purpose.
- This IS includes security measures (e.g., authentication and access controls) to protect USG interests--not for your personal benefit or privacy.
- NOTICE: There is the potential that information presented and exported from the AF Portal contains FOUO or Controlled Unclassified Information (CUI). It is the responsibility of all users to ensure information extracted from the AF Portal is appropriately marked and properly safeguarded. If you are not sure of the safeguards necessary for the information, contact your functional lead or Information Security Officer.
- Notwithstanding the above, using this IS does not constitute consent to PM, LE or CI investigative searching or monitoring of the content of privileged communications, or work product, related to personal representation or services by attorneys, psychotherapists, or clergy, and their assistants. Such communications and work product are private and confidential. See User Agreement for details.

I AGREE

SOURCE: U.S. Air Force, 2015.

Hosting the survey outside this system let airmen complete the survey without using their CAC identification cards to access the website. This meant that airmen could participate through communication channels not officially monitored by Air Force information security and law enforcement offices.

Because this survey was not a census, as is the case with the recurring Air Force Climate Survey or the Air Force Caring for People Survey, we wanted to explain how airmen were selected for the sample. We did not want airmen to think anyone had nominated them to participate based on their own behavior or others' perceptions of their social or mental well-being. To address any potential concern of targeted recruiting for the survey, we informed invitees that a computer had randomly selected them to participate. Samples can produce higher response rates than census surveys, which researchers liken to what psychologists call the "bystander effect"; that is, the presence of others decreases the likelihood that someone will help someone else in need because the would-be helper assumes that others will step in (Dillman, Smyth, and Christian, 2009, p. 273).

The invitation further specified the voluntary and confidential nature of the survey. Airmen were informed they could opt out with no negative consequences to their assignments, promotions, or benefits. We explained that no one outside the RAND project team (including Air Force leaders and health professionals) would have access to individual responses or even reports on their unit. The demographic questions on the survey were designed to provide the study sufficient information about respondent characteristics, but not at such a detailed level that airmen's identities could be deduced. The survey opened by asking only for Air Force affiliation (active duty, guard, or reserve), rank group (not specific rank), gender, and age group (not specific age). It asked about current deployment status, but it did not ask for the location or dates of deployment, nor did the survey ever ask for an airman's unit, duty station, or occupation. Other relevant demographic questions appeared toward the end of the survey: relationship status, whether the respondent had any minor children (but not their number or ages), education level, and standard DoD race and ethnicity questions.[3]

Time Frame and Reminders

The survey time frame was established to account for potential gaps in airmen's ability to receive the survey invitation or participate in the survey. Both the survey launch and the initial email invitations came at the end of June 2012. Email reminders were sent every two weeks to active-duty airmen and every month to guard and reserve airmen. The reminders began differently from the original invitation and were designed to reinforce the notion that we were not actually able to link people to their surveys, so we did not know who had completed them and who had not:

> You were previously sent the invitation below to participate in a survey about the role of the Internet, mobile phones, social media and other technologies in Airmen's lives. This reminder is being sent to all invitees who did not choose to opt out of follow-up survey reminders.
>
> If you have already completed this survey, thank you for your participation!
>
> If you have not already completed this survey, remember that it is available on the Internet and can be accessed via any computer or smartphone.

Survey participation spiked during the first few days after invitations or reminders were sent.[4] The last email reminder indicated that the survey end date was approaching. Because some guard and reserve units do not drill during the summer months (so the airmen might not check their Air Force email accounts), we kept the survey open longer for guard and reserve members. Once the survey management software indicators suggested that the final response rates would be lower than anticipated, we sent a new round of invitations to an additional sample of airmen in early August, doubling the sample size. The Air Force research sponsor preferred this option

---

[3] To review the complete survey instrument, including the informed-consent statement and demographic survey items, see Appendix A in Miller et al., 2014.

[4] The Multimode Interviewing Capability survey administration tools permit researchers to track hourly and daily participation rates.

over leaving the survey open to previous invitees, which would delay reporting the survey results to the Air Force. The survey closed to active-duty airmen at the end of August and to guard and reserve members at the end of October.

As a result, half the active-duty survey sample had less than one month to respond to the invitation. The purpose of the additional push for respondents was to obtain a sufficient number of participants for the planned statistical analyses, which was achieved. Because we were unable to identify respondents, and because the latter survey period included both the new active-duty invitees and original invitees responding to reminders, we cannot calculate response rates for the initial set of invitees separately from those who had a much shorter window in which to respond.

Known Survey Recruiting Challenges

At the time of survey administration, the RAND survey team was aware of some potential disadvantages the survey could face with recruiting survey participants generally and expected lower response rates than was typical for highly publicized, well-known Air Force surveys.

An Unfamiliar Survey

Recurring DoD surveys can establish name recognition and a survey reputation, which could be beneficial for recruiting participants. AFPC has worked to build on both to encourage participation in the Air Force Climate Survey. It can point airmen to examples of changes that resulted from prior surveys as evidence that taking surveys can make a difference. Because it is familiar, airmen already recognize the survey as a legitimate endeavor. Of course, recurring surveys could have a negative reputation as well. Additionally, airmen could tire of being asked to complete similar surveys approximately every other year. Regardless, a well-known Air Force survey might have an advantage in an environment in which people are primed to be alert for illegitimate attempts to access sensitive information and Air Force computer networks.

Timing Disadvantages

The survey suffered from two timing disadvantages. First, because of delays beyond our control, we could not administer our survey until the summer of 2012. For a variety of reasons, administering the survey during the summer made it more challenging to reach airmen. It is common for airmen to move from one base to the next during the summer. A new duty station might also mean a new Air Force email address, making the addresses we had for survey invitations outdated. Family vacations are more common in the summer because children are out of school. And, as mentioned, guard and reserve airmen might be more difficult to reach in the summer because some units do not meet then.

The airmen in our survey sample might also have had survey fatigue. Not only did our invitations follow on the heels of the Air Force Climate Survey; they also might have been competing with other survey requests and reminders. For example, more than 32,000 guard and reserve airmen were invited to participate in DoD's SOFS from the end of June to September 10, 2012 (DMDC, 2012e, p. 19), as were about 11,000 active-duty airmen (DMDC, 2012d, p. 19). Other smaller-scale and local survey efforts might have been under way as well.

Lack of Local Advocates and Sponsors

Some large-scale surveys of military personnel can mobilize survey advocates or sponsors at the unit or installation level. These local contacts can send messages that precede or follow survey invitations to reinforce the legitimacy and value of a survey effort. The hypothesized benefit is that service members are more likely to respond more favorably to a message from someone closer to them organizationally—someone they might know and who might be more influential—than from the service's headquarters. Additionally, local advocates or sponsors can act to remove hurdles to access (e.g., set aside computers for use in taking a survey) or provide permissible incentives (e.g., announce that, if their installation achieves a 50-percent survey participation rate, all nonessential personnel can leave early on a given Friday). The Air Force Survey Office has not conducted any formal studies on the impact that local advocates have on rates of participation in the Air Force Climate Survey, but it has found that participation is greater when commanders or unit leaders send emails before and during the survey to encourage their members to participate. The value of those messages also appears to increase when leaders communicate how the results of the previous climate survey were used to make improvements. One representative from the Air Force Survey Office summarized that office's experience: "Bottom line, if members believe their leader will take the results seriously, they seem more likely to respond." This experience also echoes the experience of the lead author of this report, who has been engaged in military personnel survey research since 1992. Our survey lacked this kind of on-site advocacy.

Lack of Incentives

DoD policy presents challenges to providing incentives to military personnel: "Federal personnel participating as human subjects in DoD-conducted research while on duty may only be compensated for blood draws . . . and may not be otherwise compensated for general research participation" (Under Secretary of Defense for Acquisition, Technology, and Logistics, 2011, p. 27). Policy does permit federal personnel to receive incentives for human subjects research survey participation while they are off-duty, although payments must not come from a federal source (though payment from a federal contractor or other sources is allowed) (Under Secretary of Defense for Acquisition, Technology, and Logistics, 2011, p. 27). To offer a gift or financial incentive for airmen to participate in a military-sponsored survey, RAND would have to ensure that airmen are not completing the survey during duty hours. RAND did not pursue incentives because ensuring that only off-duty airmen completed surveys was a significant hurdle and because this requirement would have severely limited the times when airmen could participate. In a subsequent survey effort, however, RAND researchers were able to offer a token monetary gift that did not face this restriction because receipt was not conditional on survey completion and thus did not constitute compensation.

Conclusion

The RAND team employed several strategies to promote participation in the 2012 RAND ICT and well-being web-based survey of airmen. These strategies were designed to address potential security concerns about the source of the email invitations and the legitimacy of the survey itself, to assure invitees that their responses would be confidential and they could skip questions they did not care to answer, and to establish reminder messages and a survey administration timeline that would provide multiple opportunities for airmen to participate. Although a variety of factors could have lowered overall response rates, including approximately half of the survey respondents having less time to respond, sufficient numbers of participants were obtained for the planned statistical analyses of the study.

Appendix B. Survey Invitation for the 2012 RAND Survey of Airmen on Information and Communication Technologies and Well-Being

MEMORANDUM FOR: Rank/Name   Date

SUBJECT: Technologies to Promote Social and Psychological Well-Being in the Air Force Survey AF12-059SG3

You have been randomly selected by a computer to participate in a survey to help educate Air Force leadership about the role of the Internet, mobile phones, social media and other technologies in Airmen's lives.

The Air Force Surgeon General, Lt Gen Charles B. Green, has commissioned the RAND Corporation, a non-profit non-partisan research company, to conduct a pioneering survey on this topic, with the aim of helping to shape Air Force policy and the way the Air Force uses technology to support the social and mental well-being of Airmen and their families.

Should you choose to participate in this voluntary survey—and we hope you will—we will ask you some questions about what technologies you use, what you use them for, and what you think about them. We will also ask you a few questions about your own social interactions and mental health. Additionally, we will ask you about using technologies to access information and support services to enhance the social and mental fitness of yourself and others.

All of your answers will be completely confidential. No one in the Air Force will know whether you have participated in the study. No Air Force leaders or health professionals will have access to your individual responses, and none will receive reports about the responses from their units.

Your participation is very important and will help ensure that Air Force leadership correctly understands positive and negative aspects of these technologies and takes effective approaches to relevant policy and support service outreach. You may, however, opt out of the study without any negative consequences to your assignments, promotions or benefits. Also you may answer only the questions you feel comfortable answering, or stop taking the survey at any time.

The Air Force survey control number for this officially sanctioned study is: [number]. You may verify that this survey is on the list of approved surveys by visiting this Air Force web page:

[web link]

Click the link below to view a survey support memo from Air Force Deputy Surgeon General, Major General Thomas W. Travis. This link is only accessible when connected to a .mil network.

[web link]

The survey is available on the Internet and can be accessed via computer or smartphone—you do not have to be on a .mil network to access it. The survey takes approximately 15–20 minutes to complete, depending on your responses. To access the survey, use the following link: [link to survey web address]

To opt out of the survey click here: [link to opt out notification].

To opt out of future reminders, click here: [link to reminder opt out]

(NOTE: If clicking any of the links in this email does not automatically take you to the correct web page, please copy the address and paste it into your Internet browser.)

If you are unable to access the survey, please contact the survey helpdesk at [email address and phone number].

The survey will be available until August 25th for active component Airmen and October 30th for the reserve component.

PLEASE TAKE THE TECHNOLOGIES TO PROMOTE SOCIAL AND PSYCHOLOGICAL WELL-BEING IN THE AIR FORCE SURVEY TODAY!

V/R,

Laura L. Miller, PhD
Senior Social Scientist
RAND Corporation

Bibliography

AAPOR—*See* American Association for Public Opinion Research.

AFPC—*See* Air Force Personnel Center.

Air Force Personnel Center, "AF Community Assessment Ends Soon," March 24, 2011.

———, "Welcome to the Air Force Personnel Public Web Services," July 20, 2012.

American Association for Public Opinion Research, *Standard Definitions: Final Dispositions of Case Codes and Outcome Rates for Surveys*, 7th ed., 2011.

Andridge, Rebecca R., and Roderick J. A. Little, "Proxy Pattern-Mixture Analysis for Survey Nonresponse," *Journal of Official Statistics*, Vol. 27, No. 2, 2011, pp. 153–180.

Anseel, Frederik, Filip Lievens, Eveline Schollaert, and Beata Choragwicka, "Response Rates in Organizational Science, 1995–2008: A Meta-Analytic Review and Guidelines for Survey Researchers," *Journal of Business and Psychology*, Vol. 25, No. 3, September 2010, pp. 335–349.

Barr, Christopher D., Christiane Spitzmüller, and Karla K. Stuebing, "Too Stressed Out to Participate? Examining the Relation Between Stressors and Survey Response Behavior," *Journal of Occupational Health Psychology*, Vol. 13, No. 3, July 2008, pp. 232–243.

Breslau, Joshua, Eyal Aharoni, Eric R. Pedersen, and Laura L. Miller, *A Review of Research on Problematic Internet Use and Well-Being: With Recommendations for the U.S. Air Force*, Santa Monica, Calif.: RAND Corporation, RR-849-AF, 2015. As of March 23, 2015: http://www.rand.org/pubs/research_reports/RR849.html

Burks, Anh Thu, Lauren Walton, and Kelly Bristol, "Comparing Mode Choices of Demographic Subgroups Using an ABS Sampling Frame," *Survey Practice*, Vol. 7, No. 3, 2014, pp. 1–6.

Campanelli, Pamela, and Colm O'Muircheartaigh, "Interviewers, Interviewer Continuity, and Panel Survey Nonresponse," *Quality and Quantity*, Vol. 33, No. 1, February 1999, pp. 59–76.

Coughlin, Steven S., Pablo Aliaga, Shannon Barth, Stephanie Eber, Jessica Maillard, Clare M. Mahan, Han K. Kang, Aaron Schneiderman, Samar DeBakey, Patricia Vanderwolf, and Meredith Williams, "The Effectiveness of a Monetary Incentive on Response Rates in a Survey of Recent U.S. Veterans," *Survey Practice*, Vol. 4, No. 1, 2011, pp. 1–8.

Couper, Mick P., Arie Kapteyn, Matthias Schonlau, and Joachim Winter, "Noncoverage and Nonresponse in an Internet Survey," *Social Science Research*, Vol. 36, No. 1, March 2007, pp. 131–148.

Couper, Mick P., Roger Tourangeau, Frederick G. Conrad, and Chan Zhang, "The Design of Grids in Web Surveys," *Social Science Computer Review*, Vol. 31, No. 3, June 2012, pp. 322–345.

Dahlstrom, Eden, *ECAR Study of Undergraduate Students and Information Technology, 2012*, Louisville, Colo.: EDUCAUSE Center for Applied Research, September 2012.

Dahlstrom, Eden, J. D. Walker, and Charles Dziuban, *ECAR Study of Undergraduate Students and Information Technology, 2013*, Louisville, Colo.: EDUCAUSE Center for Analysis and Research, September 2013.

Davern, Michael, Donna McAlpine, Timothy J. Beebe, Jeanette Ziegenfuss, Todd Rockwood, and Kathleen Thiede Call, "Are Lower Response Rates Hazardous to Your Health Survey? An Analysis of Three State Telephone Health Surveys," *Health Services Research*, Vol. 45, No. 5, Pt. 1, October 2010, pp. 1324–1344.

Defense Manpower Data Center, *June 2012 Status of Forces Survey of Active Duty Members: Tabulations of Responses*, Alexandria, Va., Report 2012-058, 2012a.

———, *June 2012 Status of Forces Survey of Reserve Component Members: Tabulations of Responses*, Alexandria, Va., Report 2012-040, 2012b.

———, *2012 Workplace and Gender Relations Survey of Reserve Component Members: Statistical Methodology Report*, Alexandria, Va., Report 2012-052, September 2012c.

———, *June 2012 Status of Forces Survey of Active Duty Members: Statistical Methodology Report*, Alexandria, Va., Report 2012-057, September 2012d.

———, *June 2012 Status of Forces Survey of Reserve Component Members: Statistical Methodology Report*, Alexandria, Va., Report 2012-042, October 2012e.

———, *2012 Workplace and Gender Relations Survey of Active Duty Members: Statistical Methodology Report*, Alexandria, Va., Report 2012-067, December 2012f.

———, *2012 Workplace and Gender Relations Survey of Active Duty Members: Tabulations of Responses*, Alexandria, Va., Report 2012-065, April 2013.

———, *2012 Workplace and Gender Relations Survey of Active Duty Members: Nonresponse Bias Analysis Report*, Alexandria, Va., Report 2013-059, January 2014.

Dillman, Don A., Jolene D. Smyth, and Leah Melani Christian, *Internet, Mail, and Mixed-Mode Surveys: The Tailored Design Method*, 3rd ed., Hoboken, N.J.: Wiley and Sons, 2009.

DoD—*See* U.S. Department of Defense.

Edwards, Philip James, Ian Roberts, Mike J. Clarke, Carolyn DiGuiseppi, Reinhard Wentz, Irene Kwan, Rachel Cooper, Lambert M. Felix, and Sarah Pratap, "Methods to Increase Response to Postal and Electronic Questionnaires," *Cochrane Database of Systematic Reviews*, No. 3, 2009.

Fan, Weimiao, and Zheng Yan, "Factors Affecting Response Rates of the Web Survey: A Systematic Review," *Computers in Human Behavior*, Vol. 26, No. 2, March 2010, pp. 132–139.

Fox, Susannah, and Lee Rainie, "The Web at 25 in the U.S.," Washington, D.C.: Pew Research Center, February 27, 2014.

Galea, Sandro, and Melissa Tracy, "Participation Rates in Epidemiologic Studies," *Annals of Epidemiology*, Vol. 17, No. 9, September 2007, pp. 643–653.

GAO—*See* U.S. Government Accountability Office.

Groves, Robert M., "Nonresponse Rates and Nonresponse Bias in Household Surveys," *Public Opinion Quarterly*, Vol. 70, No. 5, 2006, pp. 646–675.

Groves, Robert M., and Mick P. Couper, *Nonresponse in Household Interview Surveys*, New York: Wiley, 1998.

Groves, Robert M., and Emilia Peytcheva, "The Impact of Nonresponse Rates on Nonresponse Bias: A Meta-Analysis," *Public Opinion Quarterly*, Vol. 72, No. 2, 2008, pp. 167–189.

Groves, Robert M., Stanley Presser, and Sarah Dipko, "The Role of Topic Interest in Survey Participation Decisions," *Public Opinion Quarterly*, Vol. 68, No. 1, 2004, pp. 2–31.

Heckathorn, Douglas D., "Respondent-Driven Sampling II: Deriving Valid Population Estimates from Chain-Referral Samples of Hidden Populations," *Social Problems*, Vol. 49, No. 1, 2002, pp. 11–34.

Holbrook, Allyson L., Jon A. Krosnick, and Alison Pfent, "The Causes and Consequences of Response Rates in Surveys by the News Media and Government Contractor Survey Research Firms," in James M. Lepkowski, Clyde Tucker, J. Michael Brick, Edith de Leeuw, Lilli Japec, Paul J. Lavrakas, Michael W. Link, and Roberta L. Sangster, eds., *Advances in Telephone Survey Methodology*, Hoboken, N.J.: John Wiley and Sons, 2008, pp. 499–678.

Howe, Neil, and William Strauss, "The Next 20 Years: How Customer and Workforce Attitudes Will Evolve," *Harvard Business Review*, July 2007.

Hox, Joop, and Edith de Leeuw, "The Influence of Interviewers' Attitude and Behavior on Household Survey Nonresponse: An International Comparison," in Robert M. Groves, Don A. Dillman, John L. Eltinge, and Roderick J. A. Little, eds., *Survey Nonresponse*, New York: Wiley, 2002, pp. 103–120.

Johnson, Timothy P., and Joseph S. Wislar, "Response Rates and Nonresponse Errors in Surveys," *Journal of the American Medical Association*, Vol. 307, No. 17, May 2, 2012, pp. 1805–1806.

Jones, Shelton, Jeniffer Iriondo-Perez, Cynthia Augustine, Robert Bray, Janice Brown, and Michael Pemberton, "Designing Longitudinal Studies of Mobile Populations Such as Military Populations," *Section on Survey Research Methods*, July 30, 2007, pp. 3046–3052.

Keeter, Scott, Courtney Kennedy, Michael Dimock, Jonathan Best, and Peyton Craighill, "Gauging the Impact of Growing Nonresponse on Estimates from a National RDD Telephone Survey," *Public Opinion Quarterly*, Vol. 70, No. 5, 2006, pp. 759–779.

Kelton Global, *Surveying Strategy: Research Tactics for Engaging Millennials*, 2013.

Klesges, Robert C., J. E. Williamson, G. W. Somes, G. W. Talcott, H. A. Lando, and C. K. Haddock, "A Population Comparison of Participants and Nonparticipants in a Health Survey," *American Journal of Public Health*, Vol. 89, No. 8, August 1999, pp. 1228–1231.

Lambert, Amber D., and Angie L. Miller, "Living with Smartphones: Does Completion Device Affect Survey Responses?" *Research in Higher Education*, Vol. 56, No. 2, March 2015, pp. 166–177.

Link, Michael W., Joe Murphy, Michael F. Schober, Trent D. Buskirk, Jennifer Hunter Childs, and Casey Langer Tesfaye, *Mobile Technologies for Conducting, Augmenting, and Potentially Replacing Surveys: Report of the AAPOR Task Force on Emerging Technologies in Public Opinion Research*, Deerfield, Ill.: American Association for Public Opinion Research, April 25, 2014.

Little, Roderick J. A., and Donald B. Rubin, *Statistical Analysis with Missing Data*, 2nd ed., Hoboken, N.J.: Wiley-Interscience, 2002.

Lozar Manfreda, K., Michael Bosnjak, J. Berzelak, Iris Haas, and Vasja Vehovar, "Web Surveys Versus Other Survey Modes: A Meta-Analysis Comparing Response Rates," *International Journal of Market Research*, Vol. 50, No. 1, 2008, pp. 79–104.

Meadows, Sarah O., Laura L. Miller, and Jeremy N. V. Miles, *The Association Between Base-Area Social and Economic Characteristics and Airmen's Outcomes*, Santa Monica, Calif.: RAND Corporation, RR-132-AF, 2014. As of February 25, 2015: http://www.rand.org/pubs/research_reports/RR132.html

Medway, Rebecca L., and Jenna Fulton, "When More Gets You Less: A Meta-Analysis of the Effect of Concurrent Web Options on Mail Survey Response Rates," *Public Opinion Quarterly*, Vol. 76, No. 4, Winter 2012, pp. 733–746.

Miller, Laura L., Laurie T. Martin, Douglas Yeung, Matthew Trujillo, and Martha J. Timmer, *Information and Communication Technologies to Promote Social and Psychological Well-*

Being in the Air Force: A 2012 Survey of Airmen, Santa Monica, Calif.: RAND Corporation, RR-695-AF, 2014. As of February 25, 2015: http://www.rand.org/pubs/research_reports/RR695.html

National Research Council, Division of Behavioral and Social Sciences and Education, Committee on National Statistics, Panel on the Research Agenda for the Future of Social Science Data Collection, *Nonresponse in Social Science Surveys: A Research Agenda*, edited by Roger Tourangeau and Thomas J. Plewes, Washington, D.C.: National Academies Press, 2013.

Newell, Carol E., Paul Rosenfeld, Rorie N. Harris, and Regina L. Hindelang, "Reasons for Nonresponse on U.S. Navy Surveys: A Closer Look," *Military Psychology*, Vol. 16, No. 4, 2004, pp. 265–276.

Newell, Carol E., Kimberly P. Whittam, Zannette A. Uriell, and Yueh-Chun Kang, *Non-Response on U.S. Navy Quick Polls*, Millington, Tenn.: Navy Personnel Research, Studies, and Technology, Bureau of Naval Personnel, NPRST-TN-10-3, March 2010.

NRC—*See* National Research Council.

Office of the Deputy Assistant Secretary of Defense for Military Community and Family Policy, *2012 Demographics: Profile of the Military Community*, Washington, D.C., c. 2013.

Office of the Deputy Under Secretary of Defense for Military Community and Family Policy, *2005 Demographics Report*, Washington, D.C., c. 2006.

———, *2011 Demographics: Profile of the Military Community*, Washington, D.C., updated November 2012.

Office of Management and Budget, *Standards and Guidelines for Statistical Surveys*, Washington, D.C.: White House, September 2006. As of June 8, 2015: https://www.whitehouse.gov/sites/default/files/omb/inforeg/statpolicy/standards_stat_surveys.pdf

Olmsted, Murrey, and Kimberly Whittam, "Trust and Completion of Surveys in the U.S. Navy," presentation for the Annual Conference of the American Association for Public Opinion Research, May 2004.

OMB—*See* Office of Management and Budget.

Pew Research Center, *Millennials in Adulthood: Detached from Institutions, Networked with Friends*, Washington, D.C., March 7, 2014.

Peytchev, Andy, "Survey Breakoff," *Public Opinion Quarterly*, Vol. 73, No. 1, 2009, pp. 74–97.

Quigley, Barbara, Richard A. Riemer, Dana E. Cruzen, and Stuart Rosen, *Internet Versus Paper Survey Administration: Preliminary Finding on Response Rates*, paper presented at the 42nd annual conference of the International Military Testing Association, Edinburgh, UK, November 7–9, 2000.

Riley, Ryan, Trevor Conrad, Josh Hatfield, Heidi Keller-Glaze, and Jon J. Fallesen, *2011 Center for Army Leadership Annual Survey of Army Leadership (CASAL): Main Findings*, Fort Leavenworth, Kan.: Center for Army Leadership, Leadership Research, Assessment and Doctrine Division, Technical Report 2012-1, May 2012.

Scott, Wilbur J., David R. McCone, Lisa Sayegh, Joe Don Looney, and Robert J. Jackson, "Mixed Methods in a Post-Deployment Study of U.S. Army National Guard Soldiers," *Journal of Workplace Behavioral Health*, Vol. 26, No. 4, 2011, pp. 275–295.

Sheehan, Kim Bartel, "E-Mail Survey Response Rates: A Review," *Journal of Computer-Mediated Communication*, Vol. 6, No. 2, January 2001, pp. 1–14.

Shih, Tse-Hua, and Xitao Fan, "Comparing Response Rates from Web and Mail Surveys: A Meta-Analysis," *Field Methods*, Vol. 20, No. 3, August 2008, pp. 249–271.

Singer, Eleanor, Martin R. Frankel, and Marc B. Glassman, "The Effect of Interviewer Characteristics and Expectations on Response," *Public Opinion Quarterly*, Vol. 47, No. 1, 1983, pp. 68–83.

Spitzmüller, Christiane, Dana M. Glenn, Christopher D. Barr, Steven G. Rogelberg, and Patrick Daniel, "'If You Treat Me Right, I Reciprocate': Examining the Role of Exchange in Organizational Survey Response," *Journal of Organizational Behavior*, Vol. 27, No. 1, February 2006, pp. 19–35.

Stoop, Ineke, Jaak Billiet, Achim Koch, and Rory Fitzgerald, *Improving Survey Response: Lessons Learned from the European Social Survey*, New York: Wiley, 2010.

Tanielian, Terri, and Lisa H. Jaycox, eds., *Invisible Wounds of War: Psychological and Cognitive Injuries, Their Consequences, and Services to Assist Recovery*, Santa Monica, Calif.: RAND Corporation, MG-720-CCF, 2008. As of February 26, 2015: http://www.rand.org/pubs/monographs/MG720.html

Thompson, Lori Foster, and Eric A. Surface, "Employee Surveys Administered Online: Attitudes Toward the Medium, Nonresponse, and Data Representativeness," *Organizational Research Methods*, Vol. 10, No. 2, April 2007, pp. 241–261.

Thompson, Lori Foster, Eric A. Surface, Don L. Martin, and Michael G. Sanders, "From Paper to Pixels: Moving Personnel Surveys to the Web," *Personnel Psychology*, Vol. 56, No. 1, March 2003, pp. 197–227.

Under Secretary of Defense for Acquisition, Technology, and Logistics, *Protection of Human Subjects and Adherence to Ethical Standards in DoD-Supported Research*, Washington, D.C., Department of Defense Instruction 3216.02, November 8, 2011.

Uriell, Zannette A., and Evangeline M. Clewis, *Results of the Navy Telework and Technology Survey*, Millington, Tenn.: Navy Personnel Research Studies and Technology, May 2012. As of June 8, 2015:
http://www.dtic.mil/docs/citations/ADA560752

U.S. Air Force, "AF Portal Login," last modified February 3, 2015. As of February 27, 2015: https://www.my.af.mil/faf/FAF/fafHome.jsp

U.S. Department of Defense, *Report of the Comprehensive Review of the Issues Associated with a Repeal of "Don't Ask, Don't Tell,"* Washington, D.C., November 30, 2010.

———, *2011 Department of Defense Health Related Behaviors Survey of Active Duty Military Personnel*, Washington, D.C., February 2013.

U.S. Government Accountability Office, *Human Capital: Quality of DOD Status of Forces Surveys Could Be Improved by Performing Nonresponse Analysis of the Results*, Washington, D.C., GAO-10-751R, July 12, 2010.